MISSIONS

Standard
PUBLISHING
CINCINNATI, OHIO

Published by Standard Publishing, Cincinnati, Ohio
A division of Standex International Corporation

Credits
Cover design by Brian Fowler
Interior design by Jeff Richardson
Cover and inside illustrations by Ed Koehler
Project editors: Ruth Frederick, Bruce E. Stoker

08 07 06 05 04 03 02 5 4 3 2 1
ISBN 0-7847-1367-7
Printed in the United States of America

TABLE OF CONTENTS

Introduction 4

1 What Is a Mission? 7
Matthew 28:19

2 Old Testament Missions 13
Genesis 12:3

3 Jesus' Mission 20
Matthew 4:19

4 Witnesses 26
1 John 1:3

5 Paul's Missions 32
Romans 15:20

6 Missions in the United States 40
Romans 10:14

7 Neighbor Nations 47
Romans 10:15

8 Missions in South America 54
Psalm 47:1

9 Missions in Europe 62
2 Thessalonians 3:1

10 Missions in Asia 70
1 John 2:2

11 Missions in Africa 77
Acts 8:30, 31

12 Missions in Oceania 84
Isaiah 24:15

13 Start Where You Are 92
Psalm 67:2

INTRODUCTION

The Irish poet William Butler Yeats once said, "Education is not the filling of a pail, but the lighting of a fire." In the first temple, the tent of meeting, there was a lampstand. God's instructions were, "Tell the people of Israel to bring you pure olive oil for the lampstand, so it can be kept burning continually.... Aaron and his sons will keep the lamps burning in the Lord's presence day and night" (Exodus 27:20, 21, NLT). Today we are God's temple (1 Corinthians 3:16). And our passion, our living love for the Lord, keeps our lampstand burning before him. (See Revelation 2:4, 5.) Our job in the spiritual education of children is to light a fire, a living, growing love for God within them.

The Foundations curriculum can help light that fire. Each of our students is a temple of God. So the goal of the Foundations curriculum is to construct within children the essential foundations upon which they can build (and sustain) a loving, thriving relationship with the Lord. To do this, the Foundations curriculum provides a thorough, step-by-step, in-depth exploration of the following foundations.

Quarter 1: Studying the Bible, The Foundation for Knowing God

Quarter 2: Salvation, The Foundation for Living with God

Quarter 3: Prayer, The Foundation for Growing Closer to God

Quarter 4: Worship, The Foundation for Loving God

Quarter 5: Lordship, The Foundation for Following God

Quarter 6: Stewardship, The Foundation for Reflecting God

Quarter 7: Missions, The Foundation for Sharing God

Quarter 8: Making Peace, The Foundation for Living in Fellowship

This curriculum is intended for use with students in third through fifth grades. Each quarter is independent of the others, so they can be taught in any order. In fact, each quarter can be used as a single unit to fill in a 13-week study at any time of the year and can be followed or preceded by any other curriculum of your choice.

The following arrangement is a suggestion showing how the Foundations Curriculum can be taught in two years. Studying the Bible (September-November), Salvation (December-February), Prayer (March-May), Worship (June-August), Lordship (September-November), Stewardship (December-February), Missions (March-May), Making Peace (June-August).

WALK THROUGH A WEEK

SCRIPTURE AND GOAL

The session begins with a Scripture and a simple goal. You may use the Scripture as a memory verse if you wish, or you may use it to support the theme for the day, reading the Scripture when you gather for the first prayer.

INTRODUCTORY ACTIVITY

You can begin your introductory activity as soon as the first student arrives, guiding others to join you as they come into your room. This activity serves two purposes. First, it gives the students something fun to do from the first moment they arrive. Second, it starts thoughts and conversations about the theme of the session. Talking is encouraged. Questions are welcome. Get to know your students. Make it your goal to discover something interesting and special about each one. Let them know that their mission is to discover more about God and about how they can get to know him better every day, so that God becomes their constant companion, their treasured friend, their awesome king.

DISCOVERY RALLY

Gather the students together as a group in preparation for the Discovery centers.

What's the Good Word? This is a time to read the Scripture for the day. You may also sing a few songs if you want.

Challenge. This is a time to introduce the students to the theme for the day by making challenging statements or asking challenging questions.

Prayer. Choose a student to lead a prayer of blessing for the day's activities, asking God to open your hearts and teach everyone present.

DISCOVERY CENTERS

You will need either one teacher/facilitator for each center, or clearly written instructions that tell the students what they are to do in the center.

The way your class uses Discovery Centers will depend on how much time you have and how many students there are in your class.

- If you have a few students, go together to as many centers as you can in the time you have.
- If you have more than ten students and lots of time, divide into three groups. Send

one group to each center and let each group rotate to a different center as they finish the activity, so that each student gets to go to each center during Discovery Center time.

• If you have more than ten students, but little time, divide into groups of three. Number off, one to three in each group. Each student #1 goes to the first center, #2 goes to the second, #3 goes to the third. After each center has completed its activity, the original groups of three come back together again to tell each other what they learned in their centers.

• Or you may choose to let all three centers do the same activity. Choose the one or two activities that you think your students will enjoy most. Divide the students into groups for centers, and once they are there, do not rotate. Instead, let each group do the one or two activities you have chosen.

DEBRIEFING QUESTIONS

If you have time, gather together as a large group at the end of the session to ask and answer questions and discuss the theme and/or other issues on the students' minds.

Review the Scripture for the day.

PRAY

You or a student may close your class time in prayer.

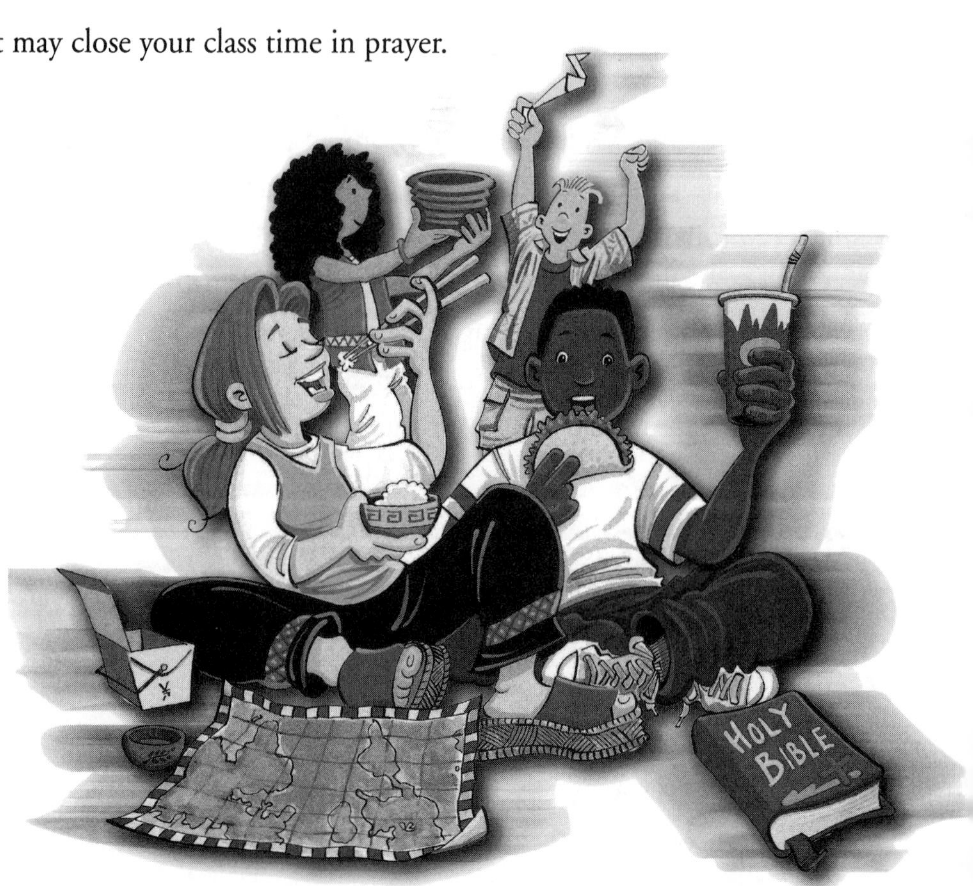

What Is a Mission?

Scripture

"Go and make disciples of all the nations."
Matthew 28:19, NLT

Goal

Learn that a mission is a goal that someone is sent out to accomplish.
Learn that God has a mission for each of us.

INTRODUCTION

For this quarter, you will need a large world map to post on the wall of your room. As your students arrive today, ask each one to find on the map a country that begins with the same letter as the student's name. When at least four students have arrived and found a country name, ask them to sit in a circle and begin a game. The first student says, "My name is _______, and I'm from _______." The student says her name and the name of the country that starts with her initial. (For example, "My name is Mary, and I'm from Morocco.") The second student says, "Her name is ______ and she's from _______ " (filling in the blanks with what the first student just said). Then the second student adds, "My name is _______, and I'm from _______," filling in his name and the country that starts with his initial. Continue around the circle with each student saying what came before, and adding his or her name and country to it. If a student forgets what another child's name or country is, other students may help by giving answers. As more students arrive, help them choose a country from the map and join the circle.

DISCOVERY RALLY

Gather the students together in a large group in front of the world map.

WHAT'S THE GOOD WORD?

Choose a student to read the Scripture for the day.

THE CHALLENGE

Tell students that the Scripture for the day was something Jesus said. Ask: **What is a disciple?** (A disciple is someone who follows someone else's teaching.) If necessary, explain that the twelve disciples were not Jesus' only disciples. Ask: **Where did Jesus want his disciples to come from?**

Point to the world map used in the introductory activity. Say: **There are 191 countries. But in many countries there are tribes who speak different languages. There are 7,327 known languages and dialects spoken around the world!**

Ask: **Does anyone know how many people there are in the world? There are more than six billion people in the world. If we all stood in line and held hands, our line of people would go around the equator 153 times! Or if our people line went out into space, we'd go sixteen times as high as the moon!**

Ask: **Do you know which country has the most people? China has over one billion two hundred million people. India has the second most, also over one billion people. The United States is third with 272 million people. And just think: God knows every one of the people in the world, and he wants every one of the people in the world to know him and be a disciple!**

Then tell your students that for the next few weeks, they will be learning about missions. In their Discovery Centers today they will find out what a mission is.

PRAYER

DISCOVERY CENTERS

1. WHAT'S MY MISSION?

MATERIALS

index cards with one of the following jobs written on each: house painter, doctor, ambulance driver, school teacher, soccer coach, car mechanic, news reporter, baker, librarian, police officer, mail carrier, airline pilot, farmer, pet store owner, pizza delivery person, fire fighter

DO: Turn the cards face down and mix them up. Each student draws a card, but doesn't show it to the others. Tell the students to give clues about the job as if they did that job themselves. For example, "I work outdoors. I use buckets and brushes. I work on houses. I work with different colors." After each clue is given, the group guesses what job the student is talking about. If the students can't guess after four clues, the clue-giver tells what the job is.

DISCUSS: Say: **A mission is a special goal. People who have these jobs have missions.** Ask students to tell you what the mission (goal) would be for the people who have the jobs listed on their cards. Say: **A Christian in any of these jobs has another mission: to tell people about Jesus. In fact, each one of us has a special mission to let others know about God, by what we say and what we do. Some people make it their full-time job to tell others about God. They may travel to other lands to accomplish their mission. What do we call them?** (Missionaries.) Ask your students if they know any missionaries. Name some who are supported by your church, and show their pictures if possible.

2. MISSION CHARADES

MATERIALS

index cards with one of the following mission jobs written on each: teaching children in schools, giving health and medical care, building houses, building roads, giving food to the poor, teaching how to be better farmers, digging wells for water, writing down a language for the first time, a Bible

DO: Ask each student to get a partner. Place the cards face down and let each pair of students draw one card. Give them a couple of minutes to plan together how they are going to act out the job on their card. Then let the pairs take turns acting out the job, with no talking, while the other students guess what the job is.

DISCUSS: Ask: **What is the main mission of a missionary?** Say: **Even though every missionary knows that their most important mission is to teach about God, many missionaries have other goals.** Ask the students to list the jobs they acted out. Let some of the students read aloud the jobs listed on any cards that were not used. Ask: **Why would a missionary spend time doing any of these jobs? Some countries don't allow missionaries. The only way missionaries can go to these countries is by going as teachers or construction workers. Other missionaries support themselves by doing other jobs.** Ask someone to read Mark 12:28-31. Ask: **How can we show love to others? How can missionaries show God's love to people of other nations?** Lead your students to understand that simply telling others about God's love is not enough. Missionaries must show God's love by loving the people in their "adopted" country. One way to show God's love is to serve people. When people see God's love through missionaries, they are willing to hear about God and his Son Jesus. If you have time, ask your students to think of some of the difficulties that missionaries might have in each of these jobs in a foreign country.

3. WHO LED THE MISSION?

MATERIALS

a Bible

DO: This game is similar to "Who Stole the Cookie from the Cookie Jar?" Students sit in a circle and number off. Begin a pat-clap pattern, first patting both hands on the lap and then clapping. Continue the pattern while saying, "Who went on the mission to Mexico? Number three went on the mission to Mexico." Then student number three says, "Who me?" You say, "Yes, you." Number three says, "Others came." You say, "Then who?" Number three says, "Number (student's choice) went on the mission to Mexico." The student whose number was called says, "Who me?" and the game continues. Try to keep questions and answers coming without breaking the rhythm. You can substitute other countries if you wish. If your church sponsors a missionary, you may want to use his or her country instead of Mexico.

DISCUSS: Ask: **What is a mission? Why would someone become a missionary? What makes a missionary different from me and you? Do you have a mission? What is your mission?** Ask someone to read Matthew 5:16. Say: **This is a mission for all of us. Whose love shows when we make right choices in the way we act and speak? How can you show God's love at school? How can you show God's love at home? How can you show God's love on your sports team? What is your mission at school, at home, and on your sports team?**

DISCOVERERS' DEBRIEFING

If you have time to review, gather as a large group and discuss your young discoverers' findings. Ask the following questions:

- **What is the most interesting thing you discovered today?**
- **What did you learn today that you did not know before?**
- **What is a mission?**
- **What is a missionary?**
- **What is the main mission of a missionary?**
- **How can missionaries show God's love to people of other nations?**
- **Do you have a mission? If so, what is it, and how do you do it?**

Review the Scripture for today.

Pray, thanking God for giving each of us a mission. Thank God for missionaries, and ask him to bless them in their missions.

Note: Give each student a copy of the "Note to Parents" (page 12) to take home today.

Dear Parent,

As you may know, we have just begun a new study of Missions. In the weeks to come, we plan to serve some foods from different nations. If your child has any food allergies, please send us a note letting us know what those allergies are. This will assist us in helping your child avoid these foods.

It is a pleasure to be able to teach your child about missions and missionaries. Thank you for helping us accomplish this task. Feel free to call with any questions.

Teacher ______________________

Phone _______________________

Old Testament Missions

Scripture

"All the families of the earth will be blessed through you." *Genesis 12:3, NLT*

Goal

Learn that even in Old Testament times, the mission of God's people was to show all the world that he is Lord and to draw all people to him.

INTRODUCTION

As students arrive, give each one a pencil and piece of paper. Ask students to write the letters of the alphabet down the left side of the paper. Then they should find countries that begin with each letter, writing the names of the countries beside that letter on their paper. They can help each other find the countries.

DISCOVERY RALLY

Gather students together in a large group in front of the world map.

WHAT'S THE GOOD WORD?

Choose a student to read the Scripture for the day.

THE CHALLENGE

Say: **The Scripture for today is something that God said to one of the first missionaries in the world, long ago. Can you guess who that was? It was Abraham.** Ask someone to read Genesis 12:1-4. Ask: **Why did Abraham leave his own country? How many people did God want to bless through Abraham?**

Tell the students that today in their Discovery Centers they will find out more about missionaries whose stories are told in the Old Testament of the Bible.

PRAYER

DISCOVERY CENTERS

1. THEN AND NOW

MATERIALS

a Bible, tracing paper or tissue paper, glue, colored pencils, tape, construction paper, copies of the Bible Times map and copies of the Our World map (pages 17, 18), the large world map hanging in your room

DO: Give each student a copy of the Our World map and a piece of construction paper. Students glue their maps onto the construction paper. Then give each student a pencil, a piece of tracing paper, and a copy of the Bible Times map. They lay the tracing paper over the Bible Times map and trace the outline of the map onto the tracing paper. Then they place the tracing paper on top of the Our World map and tape its top edge in place so that the Bible Times map becomes an overlay that shows the comparative size of what people in Bible times called "the world" and what we call "the world." If you have time, students may color the maps with colored pencils.

DISCUSS: Say: **Although the whole world was created in the beginning, people didn't live in the whole world at first.** Ask: **Where did they live?** Ask someone to read Genesis 2:8-15. Ask: **What countries are in that area today?** Help students locate this area on the large world map. Say: **From the beginning, God had a plan for the whole world. Even Adam had a mission.** Ask someone to read Genesis 1:28. Ask: **What was Adam's mission? Did God want people to leave him as they moved into all the earth, or did God want them to go with him into all the earth? God's plan from the very beginning was that everyone in all the earth would have a relationship with him. That was the mission then, and it's the mission now.**

2. WHO WAS MY MISSIONARY?

MATERIALS
Bibles, pencils, copies of Who Was My Missionary? (page 19)

DO: Give each student a Bible, a pencil, and a copy of the activity page. You may do this activity together as a group, or you may let each student work with a partner. They read the clues and guess who the person is. Then they look up the suggested Scriptures to see if their guess is right, or to find the answers if they have no guess.

DISCUSS: Ask: **Did God love only his people, the Israelites? How many people did God want to love and lead? Why did these people join God's people? Who are God's people today? Why do people join God's people today?**

3. STARWICHES

MATERIALS
a Bible, star cookie cutters, sliced bread, soft cream cheese, pimiento cheese spread, peanut butter, plastic knives, paper plates, napkins, hand cleansing gel or wipes, juice and paper cups

DO: Students should clean their hands with the gel or wipes. Then give each student a paper plate. Each student cuts out two star shaped pieces of bread. They cover one piece with their choice of spread and place the other piece on top. Before they eat, tell them that these stars represent something important. Ask someone to read Genesis 22:15-18. Ask: **Does**

this sound familiar? This is like the Scripture for today. What did God say about stars? What did God want to do in the world through Abraham and his descendents (family)? Then let the students eat their "starwiches" and drink juice while you continue the discussion.

DISCUSS: Say: **God wanted to bless the world through his people. Why?** Ask someone to read Ezekiel 37:27, 28. Say: **God wants all people to know that he is Lord. What was God's message to the people?** Read Isaiah 48:17 and Ezekiel 18:30-32.

Ask: **Is God's message different today? How many people does God want to love and lead? Why?**

DISCOVERERS' DEBRIEFING

If you have time to review, gather as a large group and discuss your young discoverers' findings. Ask the following questions:

- **What is the most interesting thing you discovered today?**
- **What did you learn today that you did not know before?**
- **Where did people live when the world began? What countries are in that area today?**
- **What was Adam's mission?**
- **Who was one of the first missionaries in the world?**
- **What did God say about stars?**
- **What did God want to do in the world through Abraham and his descendents (family)?**
- **What was God's message to people?**
- **Is God's message different today?**

Review the Scripture for today.

Pray, thanking God for having a mission and a message from the beginning. Ask him to help us spread his message today.

Bible Times Map

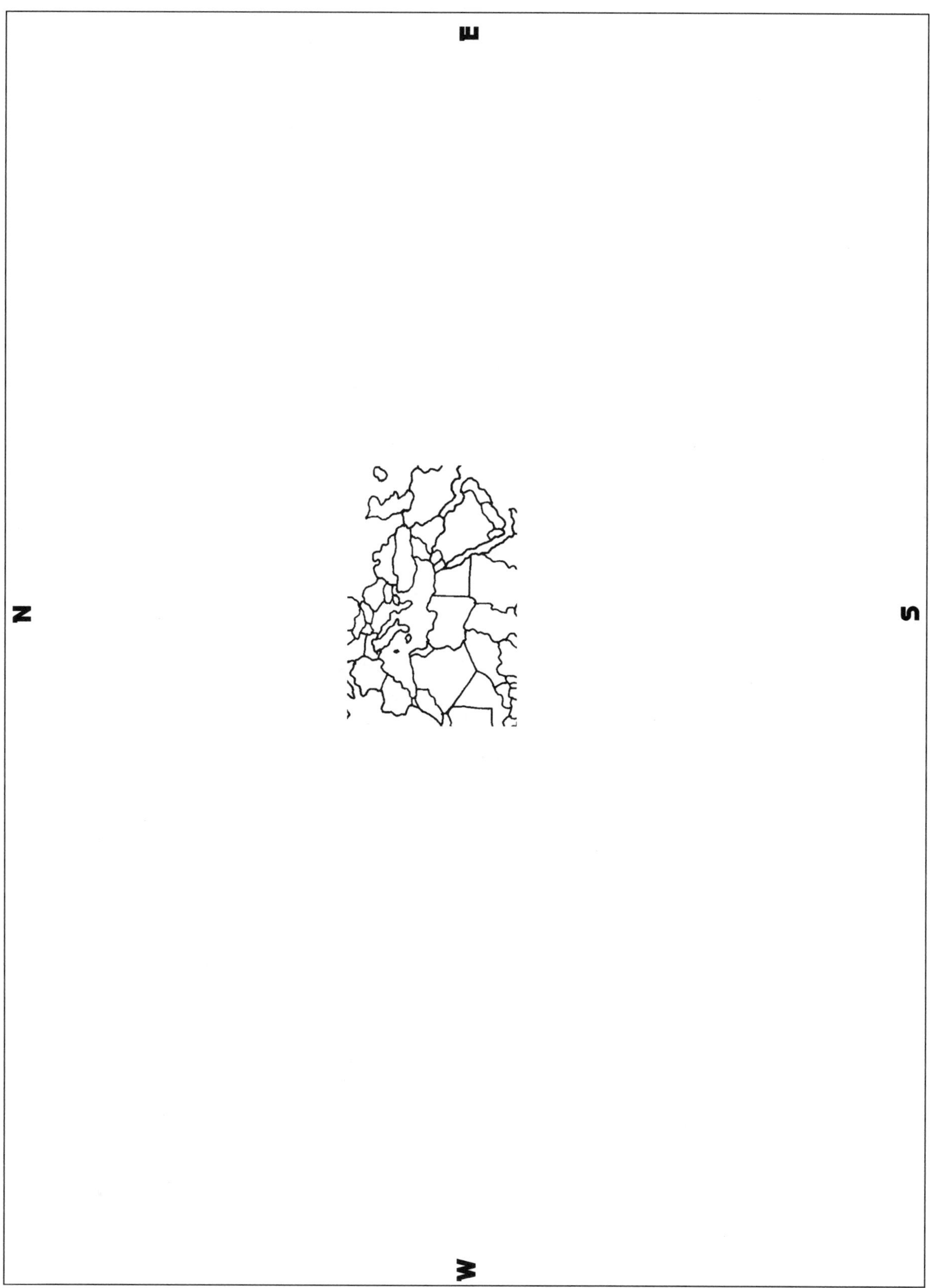

World Map

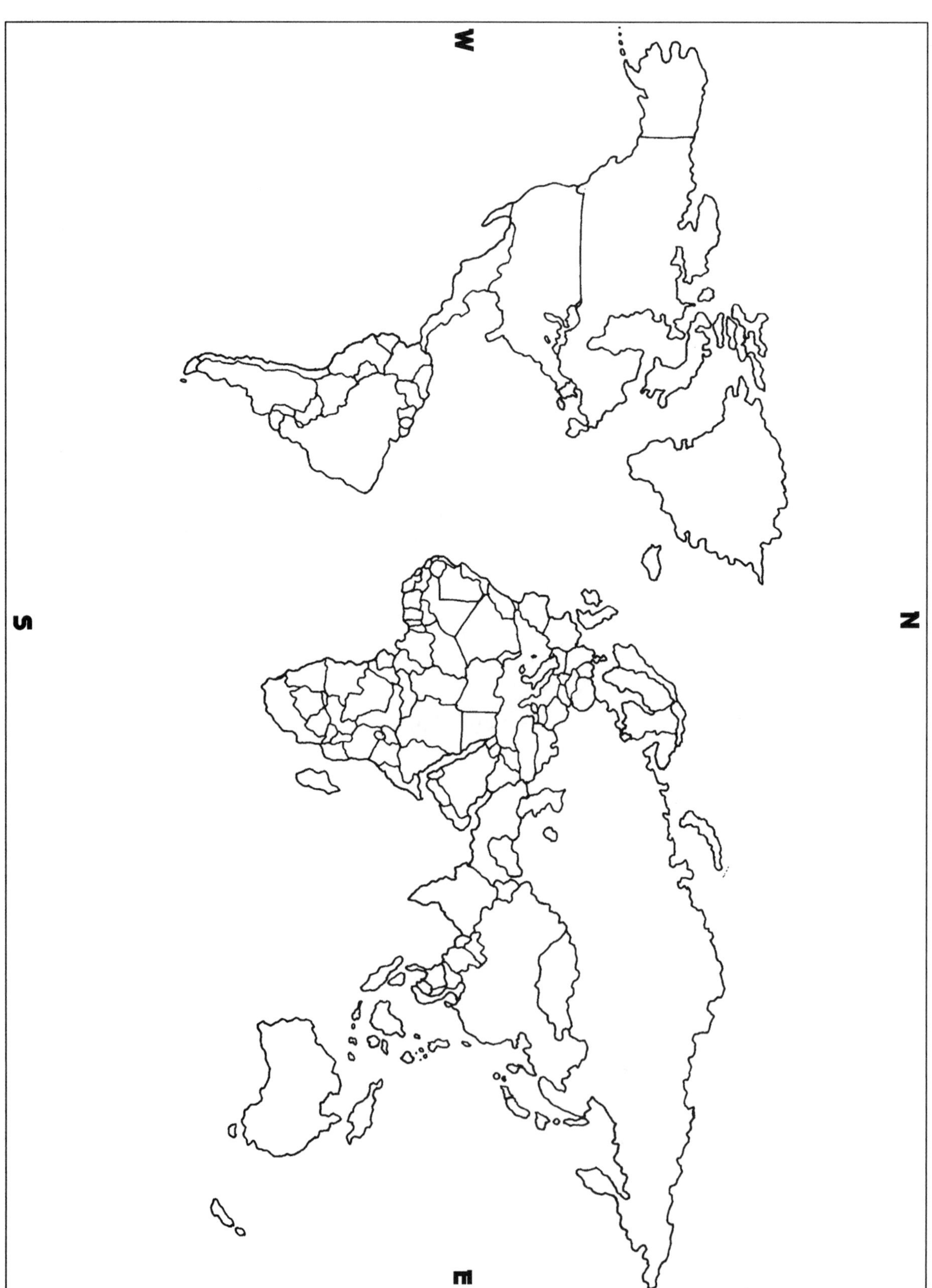

Who Was My Missionary?

"I was a woman from Canaan. Two spies sent from the people of God came to my house. I helped them hide from the king of our city. I had heard of their God, and I asked them to save my family when our city was destroyed. When the walls of my city fell, the spies rescued me and my family. We became part of God's people" (Joshua 2:1-21; 6:22, 23).

Who was I?

____

Who were my missionaries?

Two ______________

"I was a woman from the land of Moab. There I married a man whose parents were people of God. But my husband died, and my father-in-law died. Then my mother-in-law Naomi decided to move back to Bethlehem. She told me to go back to my family, but I wanted to go with her. I believed in God. So she let me join her, and I became one of God's people. I got married, and my great-grandson was King David. Jesus came through my family line" (Ruth 1:1-18; 4:13-17).

Who was I?

____

Who was my missionary?

____

"I was a commander from the land of Aram. I became very sick with leprosy. My wife had a servant girl who was one of God's people. She told me I should go see Elisha, the prophet of God. So I did. He told me to dip in the river seven times. When I dipped in the river, God healed me. I became a believer in God!" (2 Kings 5:1-16)

Who was I?

____

Who were my missionaries?

____

"I was the king of big city. One day a prophet came to us from God. God had told him to come and preach to us. At first he didn't obey. He tried to sail far away. But God sent a storm. This prophet was tossed into the sea and was swallowed by a huge fish! But God rescued him. Then he came and preached to us. He told us that if we didn't change our wrong way of life, God would destroy our city. So we told God we were sorry, and we changed our ways. And God did not destroy our city" (Jonah 3).

Who was I?

King of ______________

Who was my missionary?

____

"I was a woman who lived in Zarephath with my son. We were running out of food because of a famine in our land. One day I went out to gather sticks for a fire to cook bread from the last of our flour and oil. A man of God met me and asked me to make bread for him. So I did. And an amazing thing happened. After that day, I never ran out of flour and oil. I believed in God!" (1 Kings 17:7-16).

Who was I?

A ______________

Who was my missionary?

____

Jesus' Mission

Scripture

"Jesus called out to them, 'Come, be my disciples, and I will show you how to fish for people!'" *Matthew 4:19, NLT*

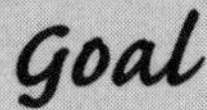

Goal

Learn that Jesus' mission was to lead us to eternal life with God.

INTRODUCTION

Before the students arrive, hang a length of butcher paper along one wall or lay it on the floor. Have crayons and colored pencils available. Also provide pictures of different kinds of fish. These could be in books or in an encyclopedia. As students arrive, ask them to find an interesting fish among the pictures and draw it on the butcher paper. This will become an ocean mural, so students can draw as many fish as they have time to draw. They can also draw and color waves and coral and other sea objects. Encourage each student to choose a kind of fish that is different from those that the other students are drawing.

DISCOVERY RALLY

Gather the students together in a large group in front of the world map.

WHAT'S THE GOOD WORD?

Choose a student to read the Scripture for the day.

THE CHALLENGE

Ask the students if any of them have ever gone fishing. Ask them to tell what it's like: Where do they fish? What kinds of fish do they catch? Who do they fish with? Ask if any of them have ever gone deep sea fishing. If so, ask how is that different from fishing in a pond or lake or river. Then ask: **What did Jesus mean when he said he would show his disciples how to fish for people?**

Tell your students that today in their Discovery Centers they will learn about Jesus' mission here on earth.

PRAYER

DISCOVERY CENTERS

1. FISHERS OF MEN

MATERIALS

manila paper, blue liquid water-based paint, disposable aluminum pie pans, sponges, old newspaper, paper towels, tape, scissors, copies of the fish patterns (page 24), a Bible

DO: Give each student a piece of manila paper, some scissors, and a copy of the fish pattern page. Students cut out the fish, put a small roll of tape on back of each fish, and stick the fish onto the manila paper. Pour enough paint in the pie pans to cover the bottoms of the pans. Students press a sponge into the paint, then onto the paper, taking care to press the paint on and around the fish. When they've finished, students carefully remove the fish to reveal the fish shape underneath.

DISCUSS: As students work, ask them to tell you what the Scripture for today is. Ask: **What did Jesus mean? How do you fish for people?** Ask someone to read Matthew 4:23-25. Ask: **What did Jesus show his disciples to do in order to fish for people?** Ask someone to read John 3:16, 17. Ask: **Why did Jesus want to fish for people?**

2. JESUS' MISSION

MATERIALS

paper, pencils, ten envelopes, a copy of Jesus' Mission (page 25)

DO: Before class, cut apart the Scriptures on the Jesus' Mission page and place one in each envelope. When your group gathers, give each student a piece of paper and a pencil. Then tell them that when someone goes on a secret mission, they often receive their instructions silently. Give each one an envelope. Say: **These envelopes contain information about what Jesus' mission was. Open the envelope and secretly look at the message inside. Then on your paper, at the top, write the words that you see in bold on the message.** After students have written the letters in bold, ask them to pass their piece of paper to the student on their right. Then they write their same message on that paper below the first message. They pass the paper to the right again. Continue in this way with each student adding his message to the paper passed to him. When the students receive their own papers back, they stop.

DISCUSS: Ask each student to read his message. Ask: **Did Jesus achieve his mission? Why or why not? Does the world still need what Jesus came to bring? Why or why not? How does Jesus achieve his mission in the world today? How can we help?**

3. FISHERMAN

MATERIALS

none

DO: Seat the students in a circle. Choose one to be the Discoverer. The Discoverer must close her eyes while you choose another student to be the Fisherman. The other students are the fish. Now the Discoverer may open her eyes. Explain that the fish must keep their eyes moving around to look at other fish and once in awhile look at the Fisherman. Meanwhile, the Fisherman looks around too, and tries to catch the eyes of one of the other students in the circle. When the Fisherman looks a fish in the eyes, he winks. Once a fish has been winked at, that fish has been "caught" and says, "I'm in" (meaning "I'm in the Fisherman's net"). Meanwhile, the Discoverer tries to find who the Fisherman is by watching for the student who is winking. If the Discoverer finds the Fisherman, the Fisherman becomes the next Discoverer. If the Discoverer doesn't find the Fisherman before all the fish are caught, let the Fisherman choose a new Discoverer.

DISCUSS: Point out that God made many different types of fish. Ask students who know about fishing: Do you fish the same way to catch all different kinds of fish? Point out that you fish for different types of fish in different ways. Ask: **Could it be that we "fish" for people in different ways too? What are some different ways to "fish" for people? Why would a person want to be "caught" by Jesus? What was Jesus' mission?**

DISCOVERERS' DEBRIEFING

If you have time to review, gather as a large group and discuss your young discoverers' findings. Ask the following questions:

- **What is the most interesting thing you discovered today?**
- **What did you learn today that you did not know before?**
- **What was Jesus' mission?**
- **What did Jesus mean when he said, "I will show you how to fish for people"?**
- **What did Jesus show his disciples to do in order to fish for people?**
- **How does Jesus achieve his mission in the world today?**
- **What are some different ways to "fish" for people?**
- **Why would a person want to be "caught" by Jesus?**

Review the Scripture for today. Pray, thanking God that he sent Jesus so that we could have eternal life. Thank him for fishing for people. Ask him to show us how to fish for people too.

Fish Patterns

Jesus' Mission

"I have come **to call sinners to turn from their sins**." Luke 5:32, NLT

"For I . . . came here not to be served, but **to serve others, and to give my life** as a ransom for many." Matthew 20:28, NLT

"Jesus replied, "Let us go . . . to the nearby villages—**so I can preach** there also. That is why I have come." Mark 1:38, NIV

"For I have come down from heaven **to do the will of God who sent me**." John 6:38, NLT

"My purpose is **to give life in all its fullness**." John 10:10, NLT

"I have come as a light to shine in this dark world, **so that all who put their trust in me will no longer remain in the darkness**." John 12:46, NLT

"I have come **to save the world**." John 12:47, NLT

"Christ Jesus came into the world **to save sinners** . . ." 1 Timothy 1:15, NLT

"Come to me, all you who are weary and carry heavy burdens, and **I will give you rest**." Matthew 11:28, NLT

"God's purpose was **to show his wisdom in all its rich variety**." Ephesians 3:10, NLT

Session 4

Witnesses

Scripture

"We are telling you about what we ourselves have actually seen and heard."
1 John 1:3a, NLT

Goal

Learn what it means to be a witness for Jesus.

INTRODUCTION

As students arrive, give each of them a pencil and a copy of Mission: Languages (page 30). They should follow the directions on the page, first copying the word "sun" in the different languages shown, then decoding the symbols at the bottom of the page to complete the sentences. While students work, place a box of extra pencils on the corner of the table. Walk around to see if anyone needs help. Then lean over the table at the corner where you've placed the pencils, and bump the pencil box so that it "accidentally" falls off and spills the pencils. Pick them up and place them in the center of the table. This will set up your challenge for today. If you prefer, you can arrange with a student ahead of time to be the one who bumps the pencil box off of the table.

DISCOVERY RALLY

Gather the students together in a large group in front of the world map.

WHAT'S THE GOOD WORD?

Choose a student to read the Scripture for the day.

THE CHALLENGE

Ask the students to tell you the words that cracked the code and filled in the blanks for the introductory activity. Then ask who saw the accident with the pencils. Tell them you are looking for a witness. Ask students to describe what they saw of the accident. Ask: **What does it mean to witness something?** (It means to see or hear something yourself, and not just have someone else tell you about it.) **What does it mean to be a witness?** (It means to tell about what you yourself have seen or heard.) **What do we usually think of when we think of witnesses?** (We think of someone who saw an accident or crime, or of a person before a judge telling what he or she saw.)

Tell the students that today in their Discovery Centers they will learn what it means to be a witness for Jesus.

PRAYER

DISCOVERY CENTERS

1. BILLBOARDS

MATERIALS
half-size pieces of poster board, markers, ads torn out of magazines and newspapers that contain familiar product slogans on them (like, "GE: We Bring Good Things to Life")

DO: Give each student a half-size piece of poster board. First read the slogans from the ads without saying the name of the company or product. Let the students guess which company or product is being advertised. Then lay the ads out so the students can refer to them. Ask them to design an ad about Jesus. They may use any of the slogans in the ads you have shown them, or they can make up their own. For example, "Jesus. Like a

Rock." "Jesus. He Likes to See You Smile." "Jesus. He Brings Good Things to Life."

DISCUSS: As the students work, ask: **How do you know about Jesus? How did the writers of the Bible know about Jesus? They were witnesses. They saw him and heard him. Is it possible for you to be a witness for Jesus? Why or why not? What have you yourself seen and heard of life with Jesus? A witness tells what he or she has seen or heard. Who can you tell?**

2. WHAT DID THEY WITNESS?

MATERIALS
pencils, Bibles, copies of What Did They Witness? (page 31)

DO: Give each student a copy of the What Did They Witness? page. Guide the students to follow the instructions on the page to find the answers to the questions. You may do this as a group or individually.

DISCUSS: Go over the answers as a group. Ask: **Why do we know these things happened? Someone witnessed it, told it, and wrote it down. When we read these things, are we first-hand witnesses ourselves? We didn't actually see and hear these things. But we believe the witnesses, the ones who did see and hear these things. What do we witness (see and hear) about God and Jesus? We experience how Jesus cares for us and provides for us. We witness his answers to our prayers. When he lives within us, we experience him guiding us. We witness his goodness in our lives.**

3. WITNESS

MATERIALS
a Bible

DO: Choose one student to be the Discoverer. Choose another student to think of something people do (play baseball, work in the garden, brush your teeth, eat, swim, etc.). This student whispers the activity he selected to everyone except the Discoverer. Then the Discoverer asks a question to each of the other students in this way: "Would I witness you doing this indoors?" The Discoverer asks the question with other times or places, such as "in the summertime?" or "at a park?" or "in the city?" You may give a time limit of two or three minutes if you want. The last student who answers a question before the Discoverer guesses correctly (or before the time limit is up) becomes the next Discoverer.

DISCUSS: Ask: **What does it mean to be a witness?** Say: **God has built into the world natural witnesses to his greatness.** Ask someone to read Psalm 19:1-4. Ask: **What is the witness that these verses talk about? Who does it witness to?** Ask someone to read Romans 1:18-20. Ask: **What is the witness that these verses talk about? Who does it witness to?** Ask someone to read Acts 14:16, 17. Ask: **What is the witness that these verses talk about? Who does it witness to? Are these witnesses still around today?**

DISCOVERERS' DEBRIEFING

If you have time to review, gather as a large group and discuss your young discoverers' findings. Ask the following questions:

- **What is the most interesting thing you discovered today?**
- **What did you learn today that you did not know before?**
- **What is a witness?**
- **How did the writers of the New Testament know about Jesus?**
- **What have you yourself seen and heard of life with Jesus?**
- **Who can you tell?**
- **What natural witnesses has God has built into the world?**
- **Who do these natural things witness to?**

Review the Scripture for today.

Pray, thanking God for giving us the Bible witness of those who actually saw and heard Jesus, for giving us natural witnesses of his greatness, and for allowing us to experience and witness his love in our own lives. Ask God to help us to be good witnesses for Jesus.

Mission: Languages

Missionaries to other countries usually learn the language of that country. Here is the word "sun" written in different languages. Copy each different word for "sun" in the space at the right of the word.

Chinese	日
Greek	ἥλιος
Hebrew	שֶׁמֶשׁ
French	**le soleil**
Spanish	**el sol**

A code is like a foreign language. Can you figure out what this says?

We are the ______ ______ ______ ______ ______ ______ of God.

God is our ______ ______ ______ ______ ______ ______.

We are his ______ ______ ______ ______ ______ ______ ______ ______.

A C D E F H I L M N R T Y

What Did They Witness?

Look up the Scriptures listed below to answer the questions. Then write the first letter of each answer on the blanks at the bottom to find out what each of these people was.

1. Read John 2:1-10. What did the servants see?

They saw ____ ____ ____ ____ ____ change into wine.

2. Read Matthew 8:1-3. What did this man see?

He saw Jesus heal his ____ ____ ____ ____ ____ ____ ____ .

(Hint: This is another word for "sickness.")

3. Read Luke 19:1-10. Where did this man go to see Jesus?

He saw Jesus from a ____ ____ ____ ____ .

4. Read John 3:1-3. When did this man go to see and hear Jesus?

He went to Jesus at ____ ____ ____ ____ ____ .

5. Read Acts 12:1-12. What did God help this man do?

God helped him ____ ____ ____ ____ ____ ____ .

6. Read Matthew 13:1-8. What did the people hear Jesus tell them?

People heard Jesus teach them by telling parables which is another word for ____ ____ ____ ____ ____ ____ ____ .

7. Read Matthew 1:21. What did Jesus' followers discover?

They discovered that Jesus came to ____ ____ ____ ____ them from their sins.

Write the first letter of each answer in the blanks below. Each of these people was a:

____ ____ ____ ____ ____ ____ ____

Paul's Missions

Scripture

"My ambition has always been to preach the Good News where the name of Christ has never been heard. . ." *Romans 15:20a, NLT*

Goal

Learn that Paul spent his life in missions.

INTRODUCTION

You will need an old sheet, 8"x 8" squares of fabric with different patterns, embroidery needles and thread, and scissors. Stretch the old sheet out across the floor or a table. As students arrive, give each one a threaded needle. Let students choose a square of fabric. Then help them sew the squares onto a place they've chosen on the sheet. You may want to recruit some extra adults to help with this activity. As students work, tell them that they are making a tent. Also tell them that today they will learn about a missionary who was a tentmaker. When the tent is finished, you may want to hang it or drape it in your room.

DISCOVERY RALLY

Gather the students together in a large group in front of the world map.

WHAT'S THE GOOD WORD?

Choose a student to read the Scripture for today.

THE CHALLENGE

Tell the students that the Scripture for today was something that Paul said. Say: **Paul is one of the most famous missionaries in the Bible. But Paul was not his real name. Does anyone know what his name was?** Ask someone to read Acts 8:1-3. Say: **Saul was Paul's real name. These verses tell about Saul before he believed in Jesus. What did he do? He worked against those who believed in Jesus.** Ask: **Why do you think he changed his name?** Then ask someone to read Acts 18:1-3. Ask: **What else did Paul do?** Tell the students that today in their Discovery Centers they will learn about this famous missionary.

PRAYER

DISCOVERY CENTERS

1. FIRST CENTURY TRAVEL MURAL

MATERIALS

butcher paper, crayons, cards cut out from a copy of First Century Travel (page 39), a Bible

DO: Roll out a six-foot section of butcher paper. Hang it on a wall or lay it across the floor. Draw a curved line and waves as shown below to designate land and sea. Let each student pick a travel card from your hand. Students must draw what the card talks about. For example, if the card says, "The roads were

very straight, and all of them led toward Rome," the student draws a straight road on the land with a sign post that says "To Rome." Save unused cards for your next group. If you run out of cards, shuffle and reuse them.

DISCUSS: After students have finished working on their part of the mural, ask them to sit in front of it. Let each one tell what his or her card said. Ask: **Why do you think Paul wanted to spend his life traveling and telling others about Jesus?** Ask someone to read the Scripture for today, Romans 15:20a. Ask: **If you lived in Paul's time, which kind of transportation would you have wanted to take? If you were to be a missionary today, what kind of transportation would you want to take?**

2. PAUL'S MESSAGE

MATERIALS

a copy of Paul's Travels map (page 37), message cards copied and cut apart from Paul's Message (page 38), one envelope for each message card, a pen, a Bible

DO: Before class, place each message card in an envelope, but don't seal the envelopes. Instead, tuck the flaps in. On the front of each envelope, write the name of the Bible book in which that message is contained.

Give each student an envelope. Say: **Paul traveled as a missionary to teach in many cities and countries. But he also taught by writing to these places. We have some of those letters in the Bible. In your envelopes, you will part of the message that Paul sent to the people in one of the places where he did mission work.** Now ask each student in turn to:

1. Read who the envelope is addressed to.
2. Find that place on the Paul's Travels map.
3. Read the message inside.

After all students have read their messages, ask them to place the messages back into the envelopes and tuck the flaps in. Tell the students that these are not all the letters that Paul wrote. He wrote some to specific people like Timothy and Titus. But these are the letters he wrote to the places he went on his missionary trips.

DISCUSS: Ask students to tell you the message they remember best. Ask: **Are these messages that people still need to hear today? Why or why not? If you were writing a message to our city, or to your school, what message would you say?** Ask someone to read 2 Corinthians 3:3. Say: **How are you yourself like a letter? What message do you want people to get from knowing, watching, and hearing you?**

3. FLIP AND FIND

MATERIALS
a copy of Paul's Travels map (page 37), a coin to flip, a button, a Bible

DO: Lay out the Paul's Travels map. Tell students that Paul made three missionary journeys. You will be going to cities he visited at different times on those journeys. Choose a student to place the button on Antioch in Syria. Then the student flips the coin. If it lands heads up, the student advances the button two cities along the line of travel. If it lands tails up, the button is moved only one city. Tell the student where to look in the Bible to find out how the people responded to Paul. (See the following references.) Help the student find the Scripture and read it. Then the next student flips the coin, advances the button one or two spaces, and reads the Scripture for that city. Continue in this way until all students have moved the button on the travel map.

Cyprus: Acts 13:12
Derbe: Acts 14:21
Lystra: Acts 14:8-12, 19
Iconium: Acts 14:4-6
Antioch of Pisidia: Acts 13:49, 50
Ephesus: 19:8-10, 18-20
Troas: Acts 20:7-11
Philippi: Acts 16:13-15
Thessalonica: Acts 17:4-9
Berea: Acts 17:11-14
Athens: Acts 17:16, 17, 32-34
Corinth: Acts 18:1-4
Tyre: Acts 21:4-6
Caesarea: 21:8-14
Jerusalem: Acts 21:17-19, 27, 30-33

DISCUSS: Stop the game in time to have some discussion. Ask: **Did everyone Paul taught believe in Jesus? How did different people react? Why do you think Paul became a missionary? Why do people today become missionaries?** If you have time, ask someone to read 2 Corinthians 11:24-28. Ask: **Why do you think Paul kept on traveling and teaching if it was so hard for him?**

DISCOVERERS' DEBRIEFING

If you have time to review, gather as a large group and discuss your young discoverers' findings. Ask the following questions:

- **What is the most interesting thing you discovered today?**
- **What did you learn today that you did not know before?**
- **What were roads like in Paul's time?**
- **What was transportation like in Paul's time?**
- **Besides traveling, what was another way that Paul got his message to people?**
- **How are you yourself like a letter? What message do you want people to get from knowing, watching, and hearing you?**
- **What was Paul's message?**
- **How did different people react when Paul taught them?**

Review the Scripture for today.

Pray, thanking God for Paul, his missions, and his letters. Ask God to help us take his message to people and to be living letters that lead others to him.

Paul's Travels

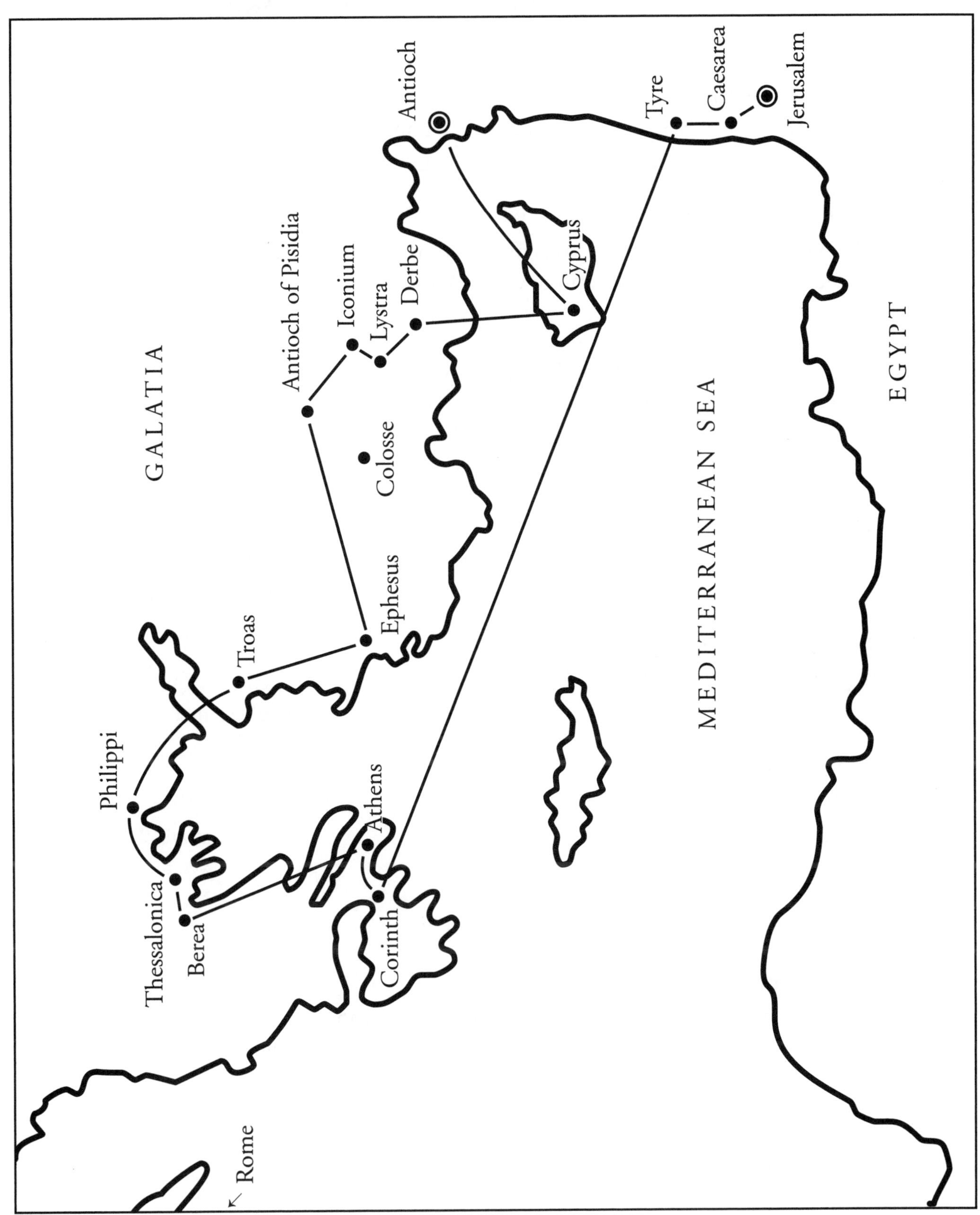

Paul's Message

To the Romans:
Everyone who believes in Jesus has a right relationship with God. This is a free gift from God. (Romans 1:16, 17)

First Letter to the Corinthians:
The message of Jesus not only saves us, but also shows us the right way to live. We no longer live like people in the world. We live in a way that will honor God. (1 Corinthians 6:19, 20)

Second Letter to the Corinthians:
People who believe in Jesus are made new. Their old lives are left behind. Now God wants us to help others come into a new life of peace with him. (2 Corinthians 5:17-19)

To the Galatians:
There is nothing we can do to earn our salvation. We are saved by faith alone. (Galatians 2:20, 21)

To the Ephesians:
We were created by God to do the good things that God planned for us to do. (Ephesians 2:8-10)

To the Philippians:
Let Jesus be your example. Serve like Jesus did, living a life of unity, purity, and joy (Ephesians 2:5)

To the Colossians:
Jesus is ruler over all. You can be complete in him. (Colossians 2:9-10)

First Letter to the Thessalonians:
Jesus will come again someday and take us all to be with him. (1 Thessalonians 4:16-18)

Second Letter to the Thessalonians:
Don't worry: Jesus has not come back to get us yet. Keep living right lives and trusting in God. (2 Thessalonians 2:2, 3; 3:5, 6)

First-Century Travel

The Romans ruled the lands that Paul traveled through. They had built roads of stone.

Stone roads were very straight, and all of them led toward Rome.

The only people who could travel the stone roads were soldiers and government officials. Other people had to use dirt paths that went beside the stone roads.

Some roads went through the countryside. These were dirt roads.

Dirt roads were packed down by the animals and people who traveled over them, and many had ruts made by carts and wagons rolling over them.

Roads could get very muddy when it rained.

Most people walked.

Some people rode donkeys or mules.

Some people rode camels.

Carts were usually pulled by oxen.

Horses pulled chariots or carriages.

Warships sailed the seas. A warship was long and narrow with two large sails. It had a row of oars close to the water on both sides so that if the wind wasn't blowing, it could still cross the sea.

Merchant ships were very common. This is probably what Paul traveled in when he sailed. These ships had large sails like warships, but these ships were wide, so they looked rounder than warships.

Merchant ships carried cargo to sell in different ports.

On ships, flags and lights were used to send signals.

Session 6

Missions in the United States

Scripture

"But how can they call on him to save them unless they believe in him? And how can they believe in him if they have never heard about him? And how can they hear about him unless someone tells them?"
Romans 10:14, NLT

Goal

Learn that there are mission opportunities in the United States. Gain a vision for giving, praying, and going to share Jesus in the United States.

INTRODUCTION

Before class, make a sheet listing the following landmarks: the Grand Canyon, the Mississippi River, the Great Lakes, the Florida Everglades, the Gulf Coast beaches, the Great Smoky Mountains, the Alaskan glaciers, Niagara Falls, the Rocky Mountains, Yellowstone National Park, the Redwood forests, Crater Lake, the Hawaiian Islands, and Kansas wheat fields. Make a copy of the list for yourself and each student. On your copy, cut apart the separate landmarks listed, and place them in inconspicuous places in your room (taped under a chair, on a shelf, etc.). As students arrive, give each one a copy of the landmarks page, and tell them to hunt for the landmarks around the room. They must not tell anyone else where they find each landmark. As they find a landmark, they check it off the list.

DISCOVERY RALLY

Gather the students together in a large group in front of the world map.

WHAT'S THE GOOD WORD?

Choose a student to read the Scripture for the day.

THE CHALLENGE

Before class, make a copy of the letter from the missionary to the Appalachians found on page 45. Put it in an envelope.

Show your students a large stew pot. Say: **The United States is sometimes called a "melting pot." Can you guess why? What might a cook put into a stew? Meat, potatoes, carrots, spices, other vegetables. These are different ingredients, but they all go together to make a stew. In the United States, people of many different nations live, work, and play together. They are all Americans.** Ask: **Can missionaries work in the United States?** Tell the students that you have a letter from some missionaries in the United States. Give the envelope to a student and ask her to read it aloud.

Tell the students that in their Discovery Centers today they will find out about mission opportunities in the United States.

PRAYER

DISCOVERY CENTERS

1. GIVE-PRAY-GO POSTERS

MATERIALS
a half page of poster board for each student, markers and crayons

DO: Give each student a half page of poster board. Ask students to write "Give-Pray-Go" across the top or bottom of the poster. Then ask students to draw a scene that would represent some part of the United States, as if they were designing a travel poster. For example, they might draw a city skyline, or a city scene, or a farm, or mountains, or the beach. They might choose to draw one of the landmarks listed in the introductory activity. When they are finished, help them hang these around your classroom or in the hallway outside your room.

DISCUSS: While the students work, tell them that "Give-Pray-Go" will be the motto of your class for the next few weeks. This motto will remind us of ways that we ourselves can be involved with missions for the rest of our lives. Say: **Every one of us can give for missions. What can we give? Every one of us can pray for missions. What can we pray? Every one of us can go somewhere on a mission for God, even if it's just next door. Some of you may be missionaries in the United States. Some of you may go to different countries on a mission for God.** Ask the students to show their posters to the group and tell about the scenes they've drawn.

2. THE MISSIONS CHAIR

MATERIALS
an audio cassette tape or CD and a player, cards copied and cut out from U.S. Missions (page 46)

NOTE: If your church supports missionaries in the U.S., you may want to use this time to let the students write letters to these missionaries. Gather the letters and send them this week. Or copy them and send them by e-mail. Perhaps your class will get a letter in reply!

DO: Place chairs in a circle, one chair per student. Stack the cards face down under one of the chairs. This chair is the "Missions Chair." Ask students to stand behind the chairs. As you play music from the tape or CD, they walk around the chairs. Stop the music at random. When the music stops, students sit in the chair that's in front of them. The student who sits in the "Missions Chair" takes the top card from the stack under the chair and reads it aloud. Then everyone stands behind their chairs again. Start the music for another round. When all the cards have been read, ask students to stay seated for the discussion.

DISCUSS: Ask: **What do these missions have in common? Why would anyone in the United States need a missionary? Why would someone choose to be a missionary in the United States when he could go to another country?** Remind the students of the letter that was read earlier. Ask: **What did you hear that was different from the way you live? What was the same? Why did these people need missionaries?**

3. A PEACE BOOKMARK

MATERIALS
markers, one 2 1/2" x 8 1/2" rectangle of poster board for each student, a Bible

DO: Give each student a rectangle of poster board. Ask them to write "PEACE" at the top on the front and their name on the top of the back side. Then tell them that each week they will write the word "peace" in a different language until they have at least seven different languages represented. This week it's in English, because that's the main language spoken in the U.S. But there are other languages spoken in the U.S. So ask them to add the Navaho Indian word for peace: hozho (pronounced hoh-zho). They can write "Navaho" in small letters under the word to help them remember what language it is. They should leave their bookmarks with you so that you can have them ready for next week.

DISCUSS: Remind the students that Jesus called missions "fishing for people." Ask: **What equipment is needed for fishing?** When someone says, "Bait," ask: **What do fishermen use as bait?** Then ask: **What did Jesus use as "bait" when fishing for people? Jesus used love, respect, friendship.** Ask someone to read Galatians 5:22, 23. Suggest that when these character qualities show in our lives, they draw people to Jesus. Ask: **How do we show love in our lives? Joy? Peace? Patience? Kindness? Goodness? Faithfulness? Gentleness? Self-control? Why would these things draw people to Jesus?**

DISCOVERERS' DEBRIEFING

If you have time to review, gather as a large group and discuss your young discoverers' findings. Ask the following questions:

- **What is the most interesting thing you discovered today?**
- **What did you learn today that you did not know before?**
- **What is our motto for the next few weeks? (Give-Pray-Go)**
- **What can we give? What can we pray? Where can we go?**
- **Why would anyone in the United States need a missionary?**
- **What did Jesus use as "bait" when fishing for people?**
- **How can we show love, joy, and peace in our lives?**
- **Why would these things draw people to Jesus?**

Review the Scripture for today.

Pray, thanking God for the United States and the opportunities for missions that exist in the U.S. Ask God to show us how to Give-Pray-Go.

Dear friends,

Our family lives in the country in East Tennessee. We are missionaries here. We love this area because it is so beautiful. There are lots of things to do. This is a part of the country that is rich in culture and language, and we like getting to know these things. For example, when a person is happy to do a favor for you, they might say, "I don't care a bit to do that for you." We had to get used to that, because at first it sounded like they were not willing to do the favor. But it really meant they did want to do it. Another saying we've gotten used to is people calling everyone, male or female, "Buddy." People use this whether they know your name or not, and now it sounds normal for us to hear it.

We have friends our age here. We love to go fishing, hiking, and picnicking with them. Sometimes we have sleepovers and birthday parties. And sometimes we are invited to pig roasts. Someone cooks a pig, head and all, with an apple in its mouth. Then neighbors from far and near come to share. They bring other dishes with them, and when everyone is finished eating, often local bands will play gospel music. Some of the instruments they use are banjos, guitars, fiddles, and sometimes a hammer dulcimer.

Our house is a log home which we are building ourselves. We had tree trunks brought to our property. Then a man sawed them into logs. We helped stack the logs to make the shell of our house. Our only heat is a wood stove. Most of our neighbors heat their houses that way too. One of our chores is to chop wood for the stove.

Besides telling others about Jesus, we help out in lots of other ways. Because of the wood and coal heat, people's homes often burn down. We have helped several families who have lost everything they owned in a fire. Last year our dad helped put out an underbrush fire that was close to some of our neighbors' homes. Dad is a school teacher. He has campouts on our property with young boys who may not ever get to go camping. Dad helps them have a good time, and also listens to them talk about their problems. He helps with an after-school program for kids who are interested in fun activities.

There are lots of ways to serve God in the United States. We are still learning what it means to be missionaries here.

God bless you,
Amy, Lauren, and Caitlyn
Jellico, Tennessee

U.S. Missions

I work with children in the inner cities. These cities are so big that some of these children have never been outside the city. They have never seen real cows or horses or mountains or forests or fields. Many of them only have one parent, and they may live in dangerous places. I tell them about Jesus and try to help them with their problems.

I work on a reservation with Native Americans. Many of them are very poor. I teach them about Jesus, and I try to help them learn good health habits. I try to help the children with their school work too.

I work with homeless men, women, and children. I try to help them find jobs and a place to live. I organize meals for them so they can have something to eat. When it's their birthday, I try to bring a cake and a gift. Some of them have never had a birthday cake before. I try to gather clothes for them, especially when the weather gets cold. I also tell them about Jesus.

I work with students who come to the United States from different countries. They are new here, and they are looking for friends. So I try to get families to "adopt" a student. These families invite the students into their homes for meals, especially at holiday times. They become friends for these students, and they get to tell them about Jesus. Then when these students go back to their own countries, they can take the good news about Jesus back with them.

I work with children who are having a hard time with their studies at school. I help them learn math or reading skills. I become their good friend. I share the love of Jesus with them.

Session 7

Neighbor Nations

Scripture

Add to last week's verse: "And how will anyone go and tell them without being sent? That is what the Scriptures mean when they say, 'How beautiful are the feet of those who bring good news!'" Romans 10:15, NLT

Goal

Gain a vision for giving, praying, and going to share Jesus in Canada, Mexico, Central America, and the Caribbean. Learn that the missions message is spread more through actions than words.

INTRODUCTION

As students arrive, give each of them a pencil and a copy of Where Can You Go From the USA? (page 53). Tell them to follow the directions, working from 1 to 10, filling in the blanks with letters found in the word above the blanks. They will be writing the names of several nations.

DISCOVERY RALLY

Gather the students together in a large group in front of the world map.

WHAT'S THE GOOD WORD?

Choose a student to read the Scripture for the day.

THE CHALLENGE

Before class, make a copy of the letter from the missionary to Mexico found on page 52. Put it in an envelope.

If you've received any e-mails or letters from missionaries to whom you wrote last week, read their response at this time.

Ask the students what your class motto is. Give-Pray-Go. Ask them to think of the map of the USA. Ask: **Which countries are neighbor nations to the U.S.? Which is north? Which is south?** Now ask students to guess which of these countries each of the following facts is about.

- **Which is the second largest country in the world? Canada**
- **Which has two official languages? Canada: English and French**
- **Which has a unit of money called a peso? Mexico**
- **Which has great forests from which they produce paper? Canada**
- **Which has the largest city in the world? Mexico: Mexico City**
- **Which grows bananas, sugar cane, and coffee beans? Mexico**
- **Which stretches into the Arctic Ocean? Canada**
- **To which would you go if you wanted to see a bullfight? Mexico**
- **To which would you go if you wanted to ride on a dog sled? Canada**
- **Which stretches along the Gulf of Mexico? Mexico**

Now tell the students that you have a letter to them from missionaries to Mexico. Give the envelope to a student and have him read the letter aloud.

Tell the students that in their Discovery Centers today they will look at Canada and Mexico as places where they might give, pray, and go.

PRAYER

DISCOVERY CENTERS

NOTE: If your church supports missionaries in Canada, Mexico, Central America, or the Caribbean, you may want to change the activity in Center #2 or Center #3, and use one of these centers to let the students write letters to these missionaries. Gather the letters and send them this week. Or copy them and send them by e-mail. Perhaps your class will get a letter in reply!

1. PEACE BOOKMARK

MATERIALS
bookmarks that the students made last week, markers, a piece of paper and marker for yourself

DO: Give the students the bookmarks they made last week. On a piece of paper, write "paix." Tell the students that this is the French word for "peace." It is pronounced "pay." Ask the students to say the word with you. Then ask them to write it on their bookmark. Gather the bookmarks and keep them for next week. Then help students learn how to say, "Hello, my name is. . ." in French: "Bonjour. Je m'apelle (your name)." This is pronounced: "Bone-zhoor'. Zhu' mah pel." Practice saying this together. Then choose one student to go first. This student turns to the person on his left and says, "Bonjour. Je m'apelle (his name)." The student who received this greeting says, "Bonjour." Then that student turns to the person on her left and says, "Bonjour. Je m'apelle (her name)." Continue this way around the group.

DISCUSS: Say: **French is spoken most often in the part of Canada known as Quebec. Most of the rest of Canada speaks English. Would it be a good idea to learn French if you were going to be a missionary to Quebec? Why or why not? If you don't go to Canada, what can you do to help people there learn about Jesus? You can give and pray. How would you tell Canadians about Jesus?** Remind students that how we act often speaks louder than what we say, so a major part of any missions work is showing the love of Jesus through the lives of the missionaries. Ask: **How can a missionary's actions share the message of Jesus?**

If your church supports missionaries in Canada, this is a good time to talk about who they are. Show pictures of them if possible. Find their location on a map. Give a report about what God is doing in their area.

2. WEAVING

MATERIALS
construction paper, stapler and staples, sixteen 8" x 1" strips of various colors of cloth for each student

DO: Give each student a piece of construction paper and eight strips of cloth. Tell the students to lay the strips side by side on top of the construction paper. Staple one end of each strip to the paper. Then give each student eight more strips of cloth. They weave one new strip under and over, under and over close to the stapled end of the first strips. The next strip, they weave over and under, over and under close to the strip they just wove. Continue weaving each strip. When all strips are woven, staple the opposite ends of the first layer of strips.

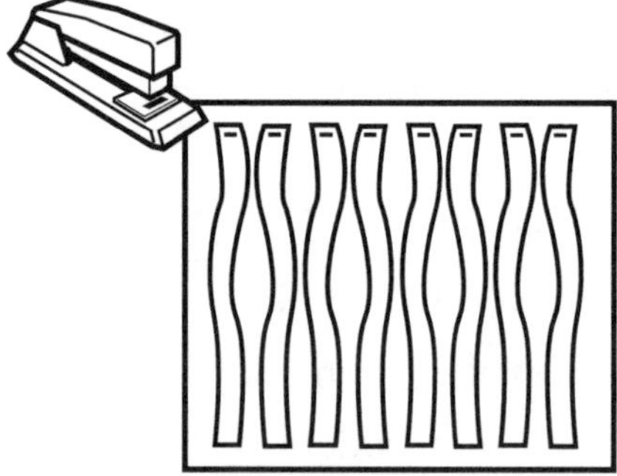
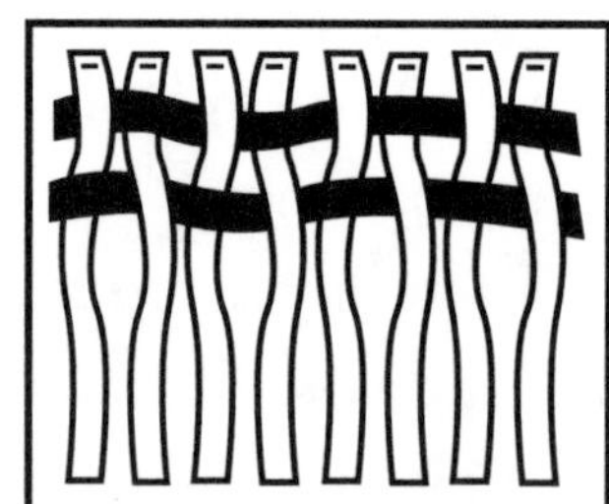
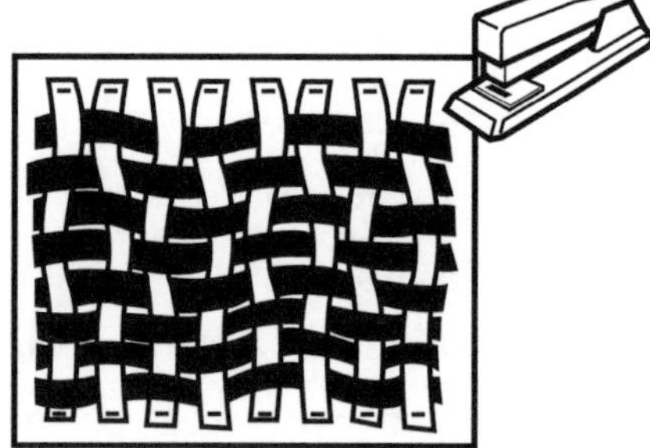

DISCUSS: Tell students that beautiful cloth weavings are commonly made in Mexico, Central America, and the Caribbean Islands. Help students locate these nations on the world map. Ask: **Why does God want people in these nations to know about Jesus? How can a missionary's life share the message of Jesus? How can we help to spread God's good news to these nations? Give-Pray-Go.**

3. DAILY BREAD OF MEXICO

MATERIALS
flour tortillas, strings of cheese, paper towels, salsa, a plastic spoon, microwave oven (optional), paper plates, hand cleansing gel or wipes

DO: Ask the students to clean their hands with gel or wipes. Give each student a paper plate, a tortilla, and a string of cheese. The students roll the cheese up in the tortilla. If you have a microwave oven, ask the students to roll a paper towel around this tortilla "wrap." Then microwave it for 15 to 20 seconds on high to soften the cheese. Spoon a bit of salsa onto each student's plate. They may then eat these wraps, dipping them in salsa if they wish.

DISCUSS: Ask the students to tell you about other Mexican foods they may have eaten. Point out that taking a missions trip to another country can be an adventure. Say: **You may get to try foods that you never tasted before.** Ask: **Why do different countries serve different foods? Countries developed their own special kinds of food because of what grew naturally in their area of the world.** Ask: **What else might you experience differently in a different country? If you were going to be a missionary to any of these countries, what would you need to know about the country and its people before you went? What would you tell the person from Mexico about Jesus? Why would your actions be more important than your words?**

DISCOVERERS' DEBRIEFING

If you have time to review, gather as a large group and discuss your young discoverers' findings. Ask the following questions:

- **What is the most interesting thing you discovered today?**
- **What did you learn today that you did not know before?**
- **Name some of the nations you learned about today.**
- **How can we help to spread God's good news to these nations?**
- **If you went, how would you tell these people about Jesus?**
- **Why does God want people in these nations to know about Jesus?**
- **Why are a missionary's actions more important than words?**

Review the Scripture for today.

Pray, thanking God for the people of Canada, Mexico, Central America, and the Caribbean Islands. Ask God to draw these nations to Jesus. If your church supports missionaries in these nations, this is a good time to pray for them as well.

Dear friends,

My parents and I are missionaries to the Mixteco Indians of Mexico. I am trying to learn the dialect that the Mixteco Indians speak. I speak Spanish, too.

What I enjoy most here is the open-air market. This is where the people go to buy all their things. We walk there, and it takes about 10 minutes. In the market there are lots of Indian ladies who sell food, clothes, shoes, chickens, turkeys, pigs, goats, and lots of other things. It is full of people in their pretty "huipiles" (long dresses), loud noises and interesting smells.

My friends and I play catch, hide and seek, and some games of Mexico. I really like to play soccer with the boys.

My favorite food here is "tacos de papa." These are fried tortillas with potato in the middle, served with lettuce, cheese, cream, and salsa on top. And I really like a kind of squash grown here that is cooked with sugar and cinnamon. You eat it by scraping it out of the shell.

The roads that lead to the villages where we work are very rocky. Sometimes we have to walk a long way to get to the people's houses. My mommy teaches English classes, and my daddy teaches stained glass classes. We also give out clothes, toys, shoes, and medicines. Sometimes teams come with doctors and other help for the people. And of course, we help the people learn about Jesus, too.

Adios from Mexico!
Your friend,
Audrey Grace
Juxtlahuaca, Oaxacha
Mexico

Where Can You Go from the USA?

Working from 1 to 10, fill in the blanks using some of the letters found in the word above the blanks. You will go around the world, making names of nations where missionaries share the love of Jesus.

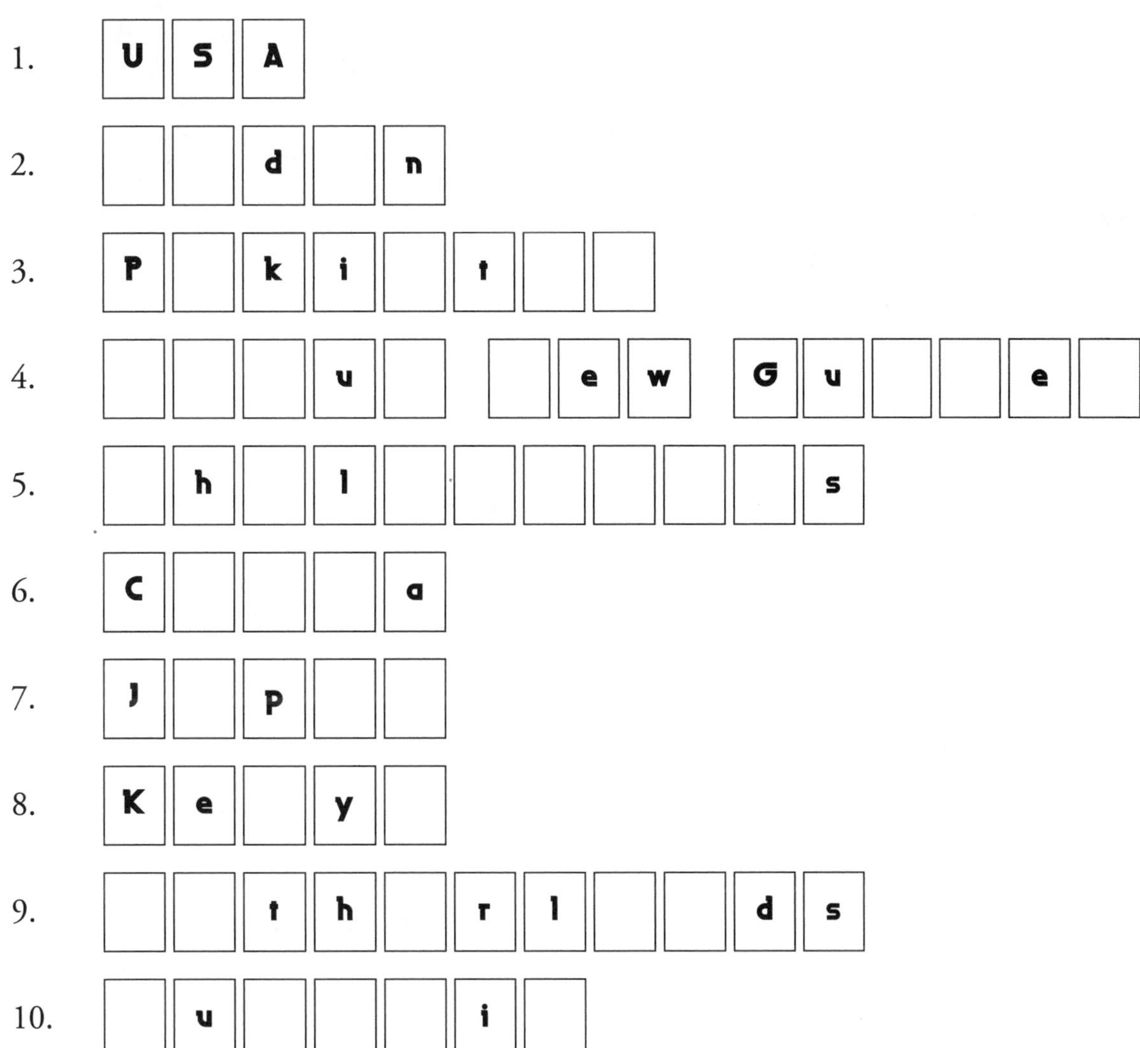

Here are the nations you will write above, listed in a different order:
Kenya, Austria, China, Netherlands, Philippines,
Papua New Guinea, Pakistan, Japan, Sudan

Session 8

Missions in South America

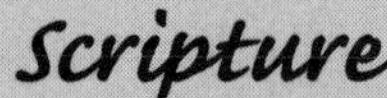

"Clap your hands, all you nations; shout to God with cries of joy." Psalm 47:1, NIV

Goal

Gain a vision for giving, praying, and going to share Jesus in South America.

Learn that missionaries respect the cultures and customs of other nations.

INTRODUCTION

As students arrive, give each one a pencil and a copy of the Picture Word Puzzles from page 60. Ask them to look at the pictures and figure out what the picture says. The first one is done for them. They write the meanings in the blanks under the pictures.

DISCOVERY RALLY

Gather the students together in a large group in front of the world map.

WHAT'S THE GOOD WORD?

Choose a student to read the Scripture for the day.

THE CHALLENGE

Before class, make a copy of the letter from the missionary found on page 61. Put it in an envelope.

Ask about the Scripture: **How many nations does God want clapping for him and shouting to him with joy? God wants all nations to clap, shout, praise, and worship him.** If you've received any e-mails or responses from missionaries your class wrote to, read them at this time.

Ask the students if their word puzzles were difficult to solve. Say: **One of the most important things that missionaries have to learn is how to communicate with the people they will be working with. Why? What might be difficult about communicating with someone from another culture? Other than language, what could make it difficult to communicate?**

Now tell the students that you have a letter from a missionary family that has no country. This missionary family lives on a ship! Give the letter to a student and ask her to read it aloud.

Tell the students that in their Discovery Centers today they will look at South America as a place where they can give, pray, and go.

PRAYER

DISCOVERY CENTERS

NOTE: If your church supports missionaries in South America, you may want to change Center #2 or Center #3, and let the students write letters to your missionaries. Gather the letters and send them this week. Or copy them and send them by e-mail. Perhaps your class will get a letter in reply!

1. PEACE BOOKMARK

MATERIALS

bookmarks from last week, markers, a piece of paper and marker for yourself

DO: Give the students their bookmarks. On a piece of paper, write "paz." Tell the students that this is the Spanish and Portuguese word for "peace." It is pronounced "pahth." Ask the students to say the word with you. Then ask them to write it on their bookmark. Gather the bookmarks and keep them for next week. Then help students learn how to say, "Hello, my name is . . ." in Spanish: "Hola. Me llamo (your name)." This is pronounced: "O'-la, may ya'-mo." Practice saying this together. Then choose one student to go first. This student turns to the person on his left and says, "Hola. Me llamo (his name)." The student who received this greeting says, "Hola." Then that student turns to the person on her left and says, "Hola. Me llamo (her name)." Continue this way around the group.

DISCUSS: Say: **Spanish and Portuguese are very much alike. Both of these languages are spoken in South America. Would it be a good idea to learn Spanish or Portuguese if you were going to be a missionary to South America? Why or why not?** Tell the students that some people of South America belong to ancient Indian tribes, and they speak their tribal languages. Say: **Besides learning the language, what other things do missionaries need to learn? They need to learn about cultural customs. Why? If you don't go to South America, what can you do to help people there learn about Jesus? You can give and pray.**

If your church supports missionaries in South America, this is a good time to talk about who they are. Show pictures of them if possible. Find their location on a map. Give a report about what God is doing in their area.

2. COIL POTS

MATERIALS
play dough (1 part water, 1 part salt, 3 parts flour), paper plates, toothpicks, bright colors of markers

DO: Give each student a paper plate and at least one cup of play dough. Ask the students to roll the dough into a few long "snake" shapes, each about the same thickness. Then they place one end of one snake in the center of the plate and begin coiling the rest of the snake around it. When they run out of one snake, they gently press the next one to the end of the previous one and continue coiling. When the coil is 3" to 4" inches wide, they should begin coiling upward, arranging one coil on top of the next. When they've run out of dough, they begin gently smoothing the dough on the outside of the pot with one hand while holding the inside of the pot in place with the other hand. Once the pot is as smooth as the student wants it, he can draw designs in the pot with the toothpick. They leave the pots on the paper plates. They can take them home to dry, or leave them in the classroom to dry and pick up next week. If students have time, they can draw colorful designs around the edges of the paper plates.

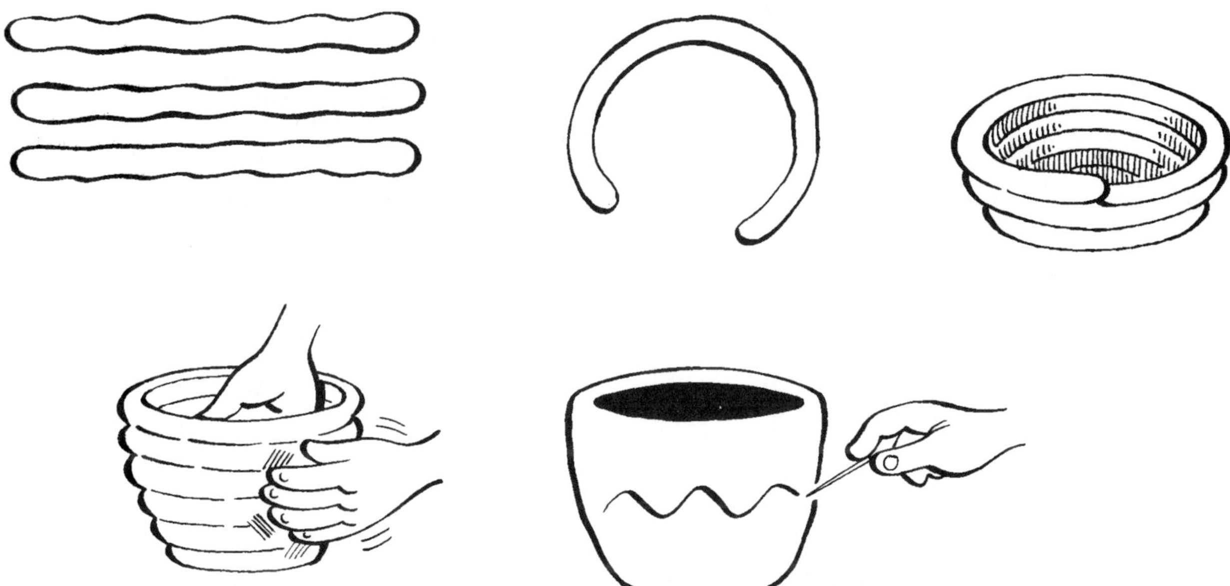

DISCUSS: As students work, tell them that it's common for many of the people in South American countries to make pottery, some with beautiful, colorful designs. Ask: **Why does God want people in these nations to know about Jesus? How can we help to spread God's good news to these nations? Give-Pray-Go. What is a missionary's main mission? Missionaries try to help**

people in other countries make a change of heart and believe in Jesus. Should missionaries also try to change the people's style of music, their customs, and their language? Why or why not? What kinds of customs might change because of the people's new faith in Jesus? What kinds of customs would not need to change? Help students understand that God welcomes all nations and languages in their variety of worship music, languages, and many of their other customs. Say: **Missionaries don't try to change other people to be exactly like them. Instead, they learn to respect customs of other nations.**

3. BEANS, RICE, AND COFFEE

MATERIALS
black beans from a can, cooked white rice, decaf coffee in a thermos, sugar, milk or cream, styrofoam cups, disposable paper or plastic bowls, plastic spoons, hand cleansing gel or wipes, paper towels

DO: Before class, cook the rice and heat the black beans. Bring them in separate containers. Also make decaf coffee (instant is fine). In class, help the students locate South America on the world map. Read the names of the countries. Ask students to clean their hands with gel or wipes. Then give the students the bowls, cups, and spoons. Let each student scoop a spoonful of rice into their bowls and then a spoonful of beans on top of the rice. Serve each student about a half cup of coffee. Students may add cream and sugar if they like.

DISCUSS: Tell the students that in the cities of South America, most people can find lots of different types of food. But this is a common meal that people out in the country might eat. Then ask the students to tell you which South American country looked or sounded most interesting to them on the map. Ask: **If you were going to be a missionary to any of these countries, what would you need to know about the country and its people before you went? What attitude would you need to have toward their customs? What would you tell the person from South America about Jesus?**

DISCOVERERS' DEBRIEFING

If you have time to review, gather as a large group and discuss your young discoverers' findings. Ask the following questions:

- **What is the most interesting thing you discovered today?**
- **What did you learn today that you did not know before?**
- **What is a missionary's main mission?**
- **How would you tell South Americans about Jesus?**
- **Why is it important for missionaries to respect the customs of other nations?**
- **What kinds of customs might change because of the people's new faith in Jesus? What kinds of customs would not need to change?**
- **If you don't go to South America, what can you do to help people there learn about Jesus? Give and pray.**

Review the Scripture for today.

Pray, asking God to draw the nations of South America to Jesus. If your church supports missionaries in South America, this is a good time to pray for them as well.

Picture Word Puzzles

Look carefully at each word puzzle to discover what it means. Then write its meaning in the blank below the puzzle. The first one is done for you.

STAND
I

    R
R O A D
    A
    D

STAND ME

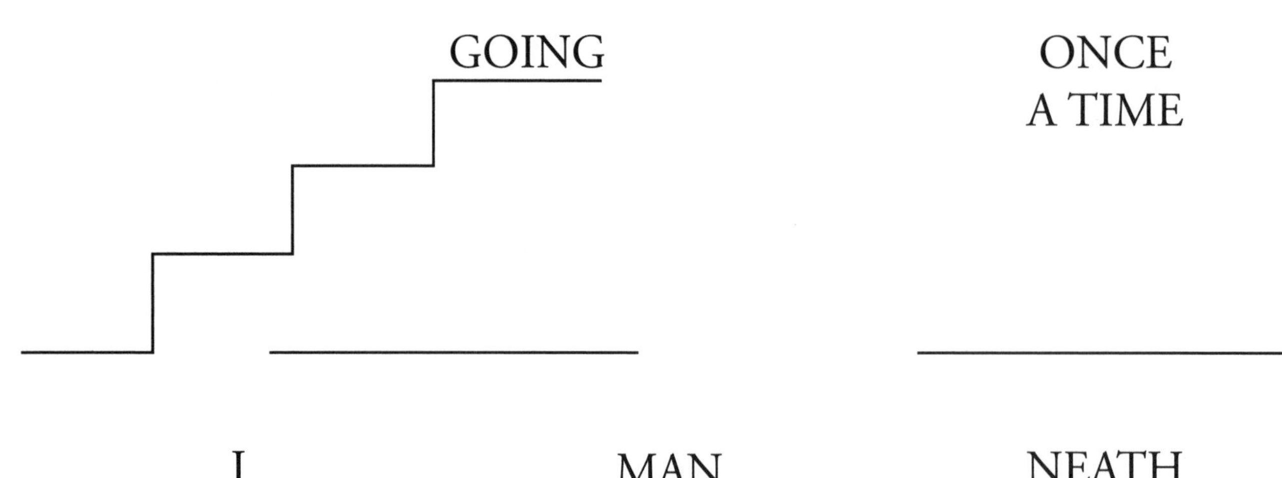

ONCE
A TIME

I
8

MAN
THE MOON

NEATH
LOOK

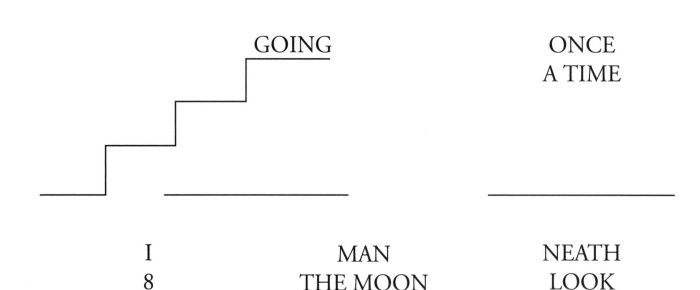

Here are the answers: I understand; crossroads; stand by me; going upstairs; once upon a time; I over ate; man on the moon; look underneath

Dear friends,

Our family lives and serves the poor and needy of the world aboard the Mercy Ship M/V Anastasis. All of our family works in missions, even though three of us are children. We've grown up on our ship, and we don't know what it's like to live on land!

On our ship, we live with nearly 400 people from 35 different nations. We spend most of the year sailing to developing nations to give out supplies. We also are a hospital. We try to touch people's physical needs as well as their spiritual needs.

We go to school on board the ship with about 60 other kids. We have a drama music group called "Ship's Kids." And we also help in the hospital ward on the ship.

Instead of going to play in the yard, we go out to play on Aft deck. To see outside, we look out the port hole. Our closest friends are from Holland, the Faroe Islands, Switzerland, New Zealand, Ghana, the United Kingdom, and of course America. The common language on board is English, but we learn different phrases and words for things from our friends.

We eat a variety of foods. Our meals are cooked in the ship's Galley. So we eat whatever they make for us. But we would always like to eat "African style," which is from a common bowl, using just our hands!

We live in one of the ship's cabins or rooms, which is smaller than some people's bedrooms. Our beds come out of the wall. But we don't mind the small room size. Of course, it means that we can't own many things. Before we get Christmas gifts, we have to clear out other things so we'll have room for the gifts!

We do lots of things besides teaching people about Jesus. We do medical and dental work. We do construction work and training and more. If you want to find out more about the Mercy Ships, go to the website at www.mercyships.com. Or maybe you could just fly over, and we'll give you a tour!

Blessings,
Blake, Celeste, and Derek
Mercy Ship Anastasis

Session 9

Missions in Europe

Scripture

"Pray first that the Lord's message will spread rapidly and be honored wherever it goes, just as when it came to you." *2 Thessalonians 3:1, NLT*

Goal

Gain a vision for giving, praying, and going to share Jesus in Europe. Learn that people may have different customs and languages, but we all have the same feelings and the same need for God.

INTRODUCTION

Before class, write the following countries and holidays on a chalk board, dry-erase board, or poster board:

Germany - Kindergarten Day, April
Italy - St. Peter's and St. Paul's Day, November
England - Boxing Day, December
France - Bastille Day, July
Netherlands - Queen's Day, April
Sweden - Midsummer's Day, June
Ireland - St. Patrick's Day, March
Scotland - St. Andrew's Day, November
Switzerland - National Day, August
Spain - Running of the Bulls, July
Greece - Flower Festival, May
Russia - Pancake Day, February
Czech Republic - May Day, May

Have scissors, tape and crayons available. Give each student two pieces of plain paper and a copy of the bell pattern from page 67. Students should tape the sheets of plain paper end to end. Then they fold this long strip accordion-style into six equal panels. Next they trace the bell pattern on the top panel. Then they cut through all six layers, being careful not to cut along the dotted lines where the pattern touches the folds. Now they unfold the bell chain. They choose six of the countries listed on the board and write one country and its holiday on each of their bells. They can color the bells if they have time.

DISCOVERY RALLY

Gather the students together in a large group in front of the world map.

WHAT'S THE GOOD WORD?

Choose a student to read the Scripture for the day.

THE CHALLENGE

Before class, make a copy of the letter from the missionary to Europe found on page 68. Fold it and place it in an envelope. If you've received any e-mails or letters from missionaries your class wrote to, read them at this time. Ask the students to look at Europe on the world map and point out some of the countries of Europe that they wrote on their bells. Ask if any European holidays were similar to ours. Ask the students what their favorite holidays are in our country. Say: **People of different nations may be different in many ways, but we all have the same feelings. We enjoy holidays. Sometimes we feel happy. Sometimes we get frustrated and angry. We all love and laugh and cry. And we all have a need for God.** Tell the students that you have a letter from a missionary in Europe. Give the envelope to a student and ask him to read it aloud. Tell the students that in their Discovery Centers today they will look at Europe as a place where they can give, pray, and go.

PRAYER

DISCOVERY CENTERS

NOTE: If your church supports missionaries in Europe, you may want to change Center #2 or Center #3, and let the students write letters to your missionaries. Gather the letters and send them this week. Or copy them and send them by e-mail. Perhaps your class will get a letter in reply!

1. PEACE BOOKMARK

MATERIALS

bookmarks from last week, markers, a piece of paper and marker for yourself, copies of the Russian alphabet from page 69

DO: Give the students their bookmarks. On a piece of paper, write "МИР." Tell the students that this is the Russian word for "peace." It is pronounced "meer." Ask the students to say the word with you. Then ask them to write it on their bookmark. Gather the bookmarks and keep them for next week. Then give each student a copy of the Russian alphabet. Ask them to write their names in Russian. If you have time, they can copy the Russian alphabet in the blanks beside the letters. Then ask them to look at the world map again and compare the sizes of some of the European nations to the size of your nation and/or state.

DISCUSS: Point out that most of the European nations speak languages different from the others. Ask the students to tell what languages some of these nations speak. Say: **Imagine that people from each state in the United States spoke a different language, used different kinds of money, and had different governments and laws. What might that be like?** Then say: **It may seem that people from other nations are different from us in many ways. But in what ways are they like us?** Say: **We were all created in the image of God, we all have similar feelings, and we were all made for a relationship with God.** If your church supports missionaries in Europe, this is a good time to talk about who they are. Show pictures of them if possible. Find their location on the map. Give a report about what God is doing in their area.

2. LA TOMBOLA

MATERIALS
paper and pencils

DO: This game is similar to Bingo. Give each student a pencil and piece of paper. Ask students to fold the paper in half. In the top half of the page, students draw a large square, then draw two lines evenly spaced down the square and two lines evenly spaced across the square, making nine smaller squares. Then they write any number they choose, one to twenty-five, in each of the squares. Now select a Caller and give him another piece of paper. The Caller, without looking at the other students' squares, slowly calls out numbers from one to twenty-five at random, and writes that number on his paper so he won't call it again during this round. When the number is called, any student who has that number in a square crosses it out. The Caller continues calling numbers until someone has crossed out all numbers in a row, column, or diagonally. That player calls, "La Tombola!" Then that player becomes the Caller.

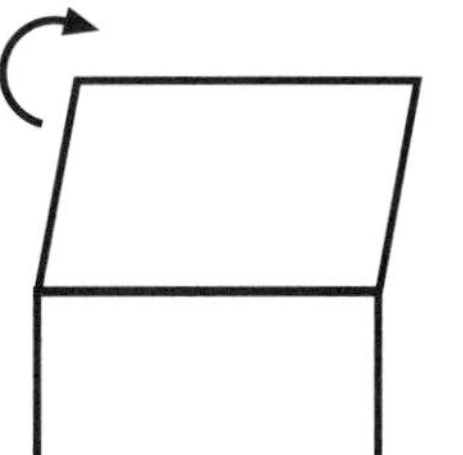

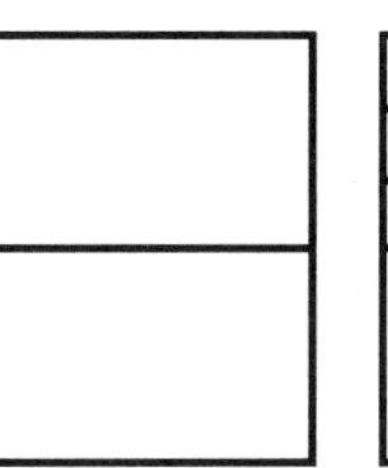

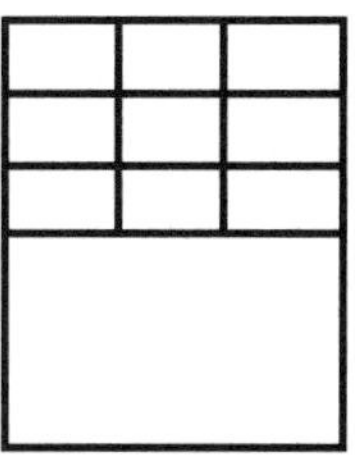

7	3	3
5	4	9
1	6	12

DISCUSS: Ask students what American game this is like. Tell them that Bingo is said to have been invented in Italy. La Tombola is its Italian name. Ask if they've played American Bingo. If they have, ask how it's different from La Tombola. Ask: **What else might missionaries find to be different in Europe? How are we like people in other countries?** Say: **We were all created in God's image, and we all need a relationship with God.** Ask: **How would you tell someone in Europe about God? What can we do to share the message of Jesus if we can't go there? We can give and pray.**

3. CHEESE

MATERIALS

seven paper plates and a marker, paper towels, hand cleansing gel or wipes, paper cups, juice, a knife for teacher's use, a variety of cheeses (as listed in the activity), a Bible

DO: Before class, write the name of one of the following countries on each paper plate, toward the outer edge of the plate, and on each plate, place the cheese that comes from that country: Switzerland—Gruyere; Greece—Feta; Holland—Edam; England—Cheddar; Germany—Muenster; Italy—Parmesan or Romano; France—Brie, Camembert, or Port du Salut. Ask the students to wash their hands with the gel or wipes. Give each student a paper towel, and slice a small bite of each cheese for them to try. Provide juice to go along with this snack.

DISCUSS: Tell the students that in some parts of the world, cheese is not a common food. But Europeans use cheese quite often in their meals. Ask which cheese is their favorite and which is their least favorite. Say: **Missionaries to other countries get to try different kinds of food. What else would missionaries find to be different in other countries? What would be the same?** Ask someone to read Genesis 1:27. Ask: **How many people living today were created in God's image?** Say: **All of us were created to have a relationship with God. What does God want our relationship with him to be? God wants to be our Heavenly Father, our Provider, our Helper and Guide. How can we help God's word go swiftly around the world?**

DISCOVERERS' DEBRIEFING

If you have time to review, gather as a large group and discuss your young discoverers' findings. Ask the following questions:

- **What is the most interesting thing you discovered today?**
- **What did you learn today that you did not know before?**
- **How are we different from or like people in European countries?**
- **How many people living today were created in God's image?**
- **What does God want our relationship with him to be?**
- **How can we help God's word go swiftly around the world?**

- **What can we do if we can't go on missions trips? Give and pray.**

Review the Scripture for today. Pray that the Lord's word will spread rapidly around the world and be honored wherever it goes. Pray that God will draw the people of Europe to Jesus.

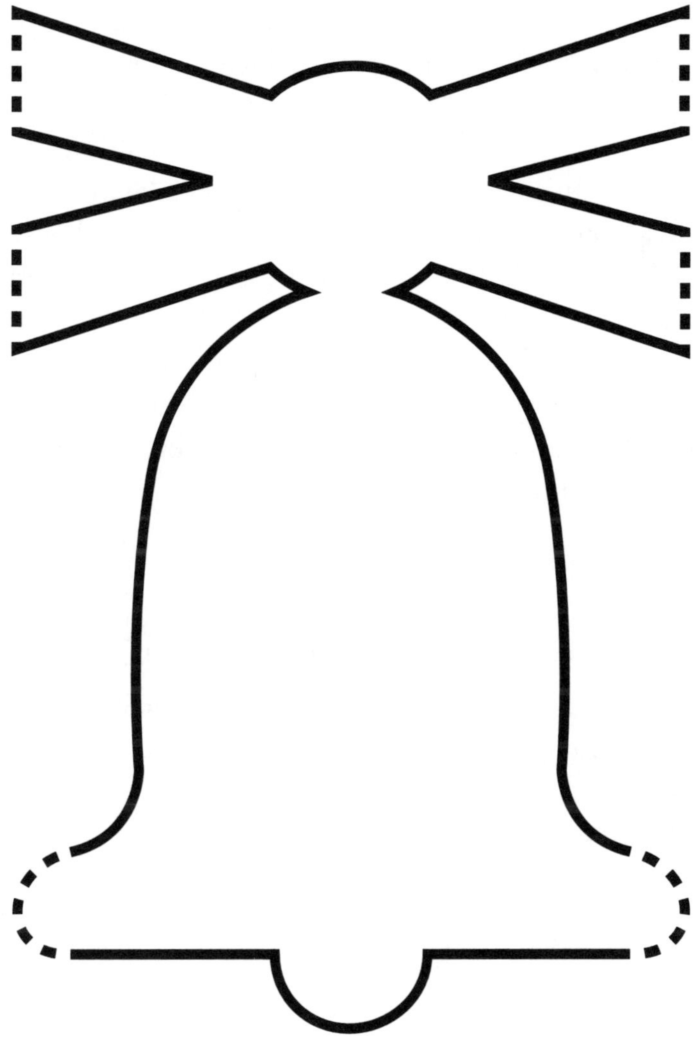

Dear friends,

Our family lives in the city of Prague in the Czech Republic. We love living in a city with lots of different ways to get around. We enjoy riding the subway, because we can look out the windows and see the river that runs through the center of the city. We also like to look at the castle that sits up on a hill across the river.

Our favorite food from this country is fruit *knedliky*. These are a kind of dumpling that's filled with fruit or fruit jam. They're boiled in water until they are cooked. They are served with melted butter poured over them, and then sprinkled with chocolate or topped with whipped cream. They are yummy!

Children here play many of the same games that children in the U.S. play. We play soccer, ride bikes, and build houses in the woods. Kids also play sports such as hockey, soccer, and Intercrosse, which is a form of LaCrosse. Often they swim, and take dance or music lessons.

Starting at about five years old, all children here take foreign languages. English is the language most kids choose. Of course, we already know English. But by the time kids here are in 5th or 6th grade, they're already studying their second foreign language. That means we'll grow up knowing three languages.

Most people here live in apartment buildings that are from eight to twelve floors high. The apartments are not very big. They usually have no more than two bedrooms. But they are plenty warm in the winter, and they take care of our basic needs.

Besides teaching about Jesus, our family teaches English, usually using the Bible. Our English classes are free, and that is usually the first thing that brings people to us. The sad thing is that not many people here realize that their problems aren't going to be solved by learning English, or getting a better job or more money. The real answers to their problems are in Jesus. So that's what we try to help them learn!

Your friends,

Luke and Andrew
Prague, Czech Republic

Russian Alphabet

Write your name in Russian. Then if you have time, you can copy the Russian alphabet in the blanks beside the letters.

Russian	Sound	Russian	Sound	Russian	Sound
а ____	ah	к ____	k	х ____	h
б ____	b	л ____	l	ц ____	ts
в ____	v	м ____	m	ч ____	ch
г ____	g	н ____	n	ш ____	sh
д ____	d	о ____	oh	щ ____	sht
е ____	eh	п ____	p	ы ____	ih
ё ____	yoh	р ____	r	э ____	air
ж ____	zh	с ____	s	ю ____	yoo
з ____	z	т ____	t	я ____	yah
и ____	ee	у ____	oo		
й ____	oy, ay, i	ф ____	f		

Two letters have no sound:
ъ called a hard sign, and
ь called a soft sign

Now write your name in Russian:________________________________

Session 10

Missions in Asia

Scripture

"He takes away not only our sins but the sins of all the world." 1 John 2:2, NLT

Goal

Gain a vision for giving, praying, and going to share Jesus in Asia. Learn that when people go with God where he wants them to go, God helps them handle unfamiliar situations.

INTRODUCTION

As students arrive, teach them how to play a variation of Jan-Ken-Pon, a Japanese game. This is similar to the game Rock, Paper, Scissors. Divide the students into pairs. One student is "even" and the other is "odd." They make a fist. Then on the count of three, they hold up one hand with a number of fingers showing from zero (closed fist) to five (five fingers up). They add the total of both players' fingers. If the total is odd, the odd player gets a point. If the total is even, the even player gets a point. They can keep score with pencil and paper.

DISCOVERY RALLY

Gather the students together in a large group in front of the world map.

WHAT'S THE GOOD WORD?

Choose a student to read the Scripture for the day.

THE CHALLENGE

If you have received any e-mails or letters from missionaries your class has written to, read them at this time.

Before class, copy the letter from Japan found on page 75. Place it in an envelope. Tell the students that you have a letter to them from Japan. Give the envelope to a student and ask him or her to open the letter and read it to the class.

Ask: **What did you hear in the letter that sounded like our country? What did you hear that sounded different? What else might be different? Which country in the world would you feel most comfortable going to? Which would you feel most uncomfortable going to?**

Tell the students that in their Discovery Centers today they will look at Asia as a place where they can give, pray, and go.

PRAYER

DISCOVERY CENTERS

NOTE: If your church supports missionaries in Asia, you may want to change Center #2 or Center #3, and let the students write letters to your missionaries. Gather the letters and send them this week. Or copy them and send them by e-mail. Perhaps your class will get a letter in reply!

1. PEACE BOOKMARK

MATERIALS
bookmarks from last week, markers, a piece of paper and marker for yourself

DO: Give the students their bookmarks. On this page is the Chinese word for "peace." Write it on your paper and show the students. Tell the students that it is pronounced "hoh ping." Ask the students to say the word with you. Then ask them to write it on their bookmark. Gather the bookmarks and keep them for next week. Then ask them to look at the world map and name some nations that are in Asia.

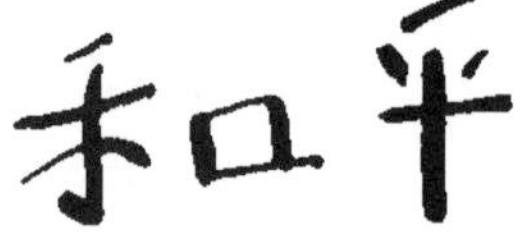

DISCUSS: Ask: **Which nations seem to be most like ours? Which seem to be most different? Do you think it would be exciting or discouraging to go to someplace that's very different? What might be exciting about it? What might be discouraging about it?** Say: **When a missionaries go with God where God wants them to go, God helps them handle unfamiliar and uncomfortable situations.**

If your church supports missionaries in Asia, this is a good time to talk about who they are. Show pictures of them if possible. Find their location on the map. Give a report about what God is doing in their area.

2. ORIGAMI

MATERIALS
plain paper cut into 8 1/2" x 8 1/2" squares

DO: Practice making an origami bird before class begins so that you can coach and help the students. Follow the directions shown on the Origami Bird page at the end of this session plan. You can refer to that page as you guide the students in folding the birds.

DISCUSS: Ask students if they've ever done any origami before. Tell them that this is the Japanese art of paper folding. People who know Origami well can fold all kinds of delicate, detailed figures. Ask: **What might be familiar or comfortable about going to Asia or any other country? What might be**

unfamiliar or uncomfortable? Why might God want people to go to uncomfortable places to tell about Jesus?

Tell your students a true story about a woman from the United States who was a short-term missionary. That means she traveled to other countries teaching about Jesus, but she stayed for only a few weeks, helping missionaries who lived there. When she was growing up, she was interested in going on missions trips, but she only wanted to go places where she thought she'd be most comfortable like Europe and Australia. She especially didn't want to go to Russia or China or Africa. She felt that these countries would be too different, and she would be uncomfortable there. But when God gave her opportunity to do mission work, he opened the door for her to go to China first, then Russia, then Africa. She went. And she found out that when people go with God where he wants them to go, he helps them handle uncomfortable and unfamiliar situations. God even helps them enjoy it!

3. EATING WITH CHOPSTICKS

MATERIALS

chopsticks, sticky rice (jasmine rice is a good kind, from the oriental food section of your supermarket), soy sauce, disposable picnic bowls, plastic forks, paper towels, styrofoam cups, green tea in a thermos, hand cleansing gel or wipes, small rubber bands

DO: Before class, cook the rice and prepare the tea. Ask students to clean their hands with gel or wipes. Then give each student a pair of chopsticks and bowl. Serve rice to the students and give them some tea to drink. They can put soy sauce on the rice if they want. Show students how to hold the chopsticks. Sometimes it helps learners to twist a rubber band around the two chopsticks at the broad end to hold them together. Students can place the tips of the chopsticks together and dip them into the rice, scooping up the rice in clumps. In true Chinese fashion, they can hold the bowl close to their chin and scoop the rice into their mouths with the chopsticks. After all students have tried to eat with chopsticks, they may have forks if they want. They can take their chopsticks home with them.

DISCUSS: Ask students if they have eaten other kinds of Oriental food. Ask them to describe it. Ask: **How is it different from American food? What might be different about life in Asia? What would make you feel comfortable? What would make you feel uncomfortable? What might be exciting about it? What might be discouraging about it? Do missionaries always have to feel comfortable in the countries they go to? Why or why not?** Say: **When missionaries go with God where he wants them to go, he helps them handle uncomfortable or difficult situations.**

DISCOVERERS' DEBRIEFING

If you have time to review, gather as a large group and discuss your young discoverers' findings. Ask the following questions:

- **What is the most interesting thing you discovered today?**
- **What did you learn today that you did not know before?**
- **What might be familiar or comfortable about going to Asia? What might be unfamiliar or uncomfortable?**
- **Do missionaries always have to feel comfortable in the countries they go to? Why or why not?**
- **Why might God want people to go to uncomfortable or unfamiliar places to tell about Jesus?**
- **When missionaries go with God where he wants them to go, what does God do for them?**

Review the Scripture for today.

Pray, asking God to draw the people of Asia to Jesus. Thank God for being with us wherever we go and helping us handle uncomfortable and unfamiliar situations.

Dear friends,

My wife and I and our four children, ages 1 - 7 are missionaries in Okinawa, Japan. The most enjoyable thing about living here is probably the scenery and environment. Japan is a very peaceful country. And Okinawa has wonderful tropical beaches and lush greenery. Though it gets hot sometimes in the summer, you can still enjoy playing outside.

The people of Okinawa are very nice and polite. They are always ready to listen to you, and whenever you visit, they always make sure they have something good for you to drink and eat.

My seven-year-old son Peter usually plays with his friends after school. They go to abacus class together, and then they play with Lego blocks. Sometimes if I let them, they play video games.

Peter's favorite food is natto rice. Natto rice is a mixture of natto (fermented beans), and rice, and a raw egg!

Probably one of the most interesting things about houses in Japan is that you have to take your shoes off at the door. You also have to sit on the floor. It might seem strange at first, but it really does help to make the home more personal and sociable.

Besides teaching other people about Jesus, we visit children at the hospital. We take them candy and toys. We tell them we hope they get better and that we are praying for them. We also visit ladies' shelters where we take their children bowling and do other fun things with them.

Japan is a good place to enjoy God's wonderful creation!

God bless you,
Chester
Okinawa, Japan

Origami Bird

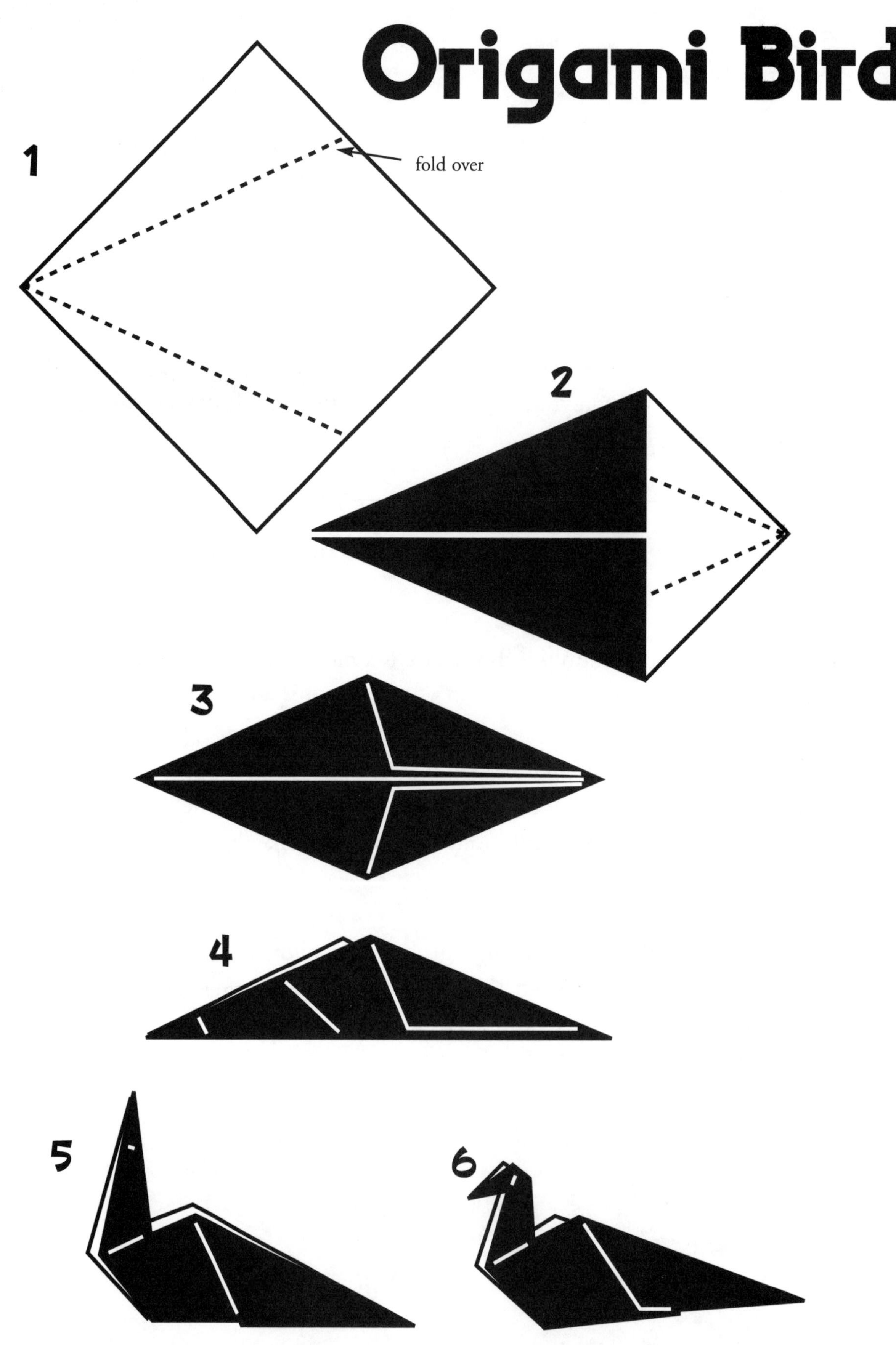

Missions in Africa

Scripture

"[Philip] asked, 'Do you understand what you are reading?' The man replied, 'How can I, when there is no one to instruct me?'"[1]
Acts 8:30, 31, NLT

Goal

Gain a vision for giving, praying, and going to share Jesus in Africa. Learn that going on missions trips not only helps other nations learn about God, but also helps the missionaries learn about God.

INTRODUCTION

Invite students to the world map. If it does not show time zones, bring an encyclopedia map or another world map that shows time zones. Tell students that there are 24 time zones. Ask why. (It takes 24 hours for the earth to turn, making one day.) Ask students to locate their time zone. Ask what time it is in their location. Point out countries in which you have missionaries or countries you have studied in past sessions. Ask students to figure out what time it is in those places. (Subtract one hour for each time zone as you move west, or add one hour for each time zone as you move east.) If your map shows the International Date Line, ask students to notice that as you cross this line, the day changes. Going west at 10:00 Sunday, it automatically becomes 10:00 Monday. The opposite occurs going east.

DISCOVERY RALLY

Gather the students together in a large group in front of the world map.

WHAT'S THE GOOD WORD?

Choose a student to read the Scripture for the day.

THE CHALLENGE

If you've received any new e-mails or letters from missionaries the class has written to, read them at this time.

Before class, copy the letter from Kenya found on page 82. Place it in an envelope. Tell the students that you have a letter to them from Kenya. Give the envelope to a student and ask him or her to open the letter and read it to the class. Ask: **What did you hear in the letter that sounded like our country? What did you hear that sounded different? What else might be different?** Review today's Scripture. Tell students that Philip was talking to a traveler from Ethiopia. Ask them where Ethiopia is. It's in Africa. So this Ethiopian man became a missionary to Africa! Tell the students that in their Discovery Centers today they will look at Africa as a place where they can give, pray, and go.

PRAYER

DISCOVERY CENTERS

NOTE: If your church supports missionaries in Africa, you may want to change Center #2 or Center #3, and let the students write letters to your missionaries. Gather the letters and send them this week. Or send them by e-mail.

1. PEACE BOOKMARK

MATERIALS

bookmarks from last week, markers, a piece of paper and marker for yourself

DO: Give the students their bookmarks. Write the word "amani" on your piece of paper. Tell the students that this is the Swahili word for "peace." Swahili is the national language of Kenya, Africa. Tell the students that this word is pronounced "ah-mahn'-ee." Ask them to say the word with you. Then ask them to write it on their bookmarks. Gather the bookmarks and keep them for next week. Then help students learn how to say, "How are you?" and "Fine": "Habari?" and "Msoori." This is pronounced: "Hah-bah'-ree" and "Mi-soo'-ree." Practice saying this together. Then choose one student to turn to the person on his left and say, "Habari?" The student who received this greeting says, "Msoori." Then that student turns to the person on her left and says, "Habari?" Continue this way around the group.

DISCUSS: If your church supports missionaries in Africa, this is a good time to talk about who they are. Give a report about what God is doing in their area. Ask: **How does missions work bless the people of the nations where the missionaries go? How can missions work bless the missionaries?** Say: **God often teaches missionaries as much or more than he teaches the people they go to. What could God teach a missionary? God can teach them to depend on him. He can teach them that people who are poor can be rich in faith. He can teach them that life's importance is in people, not things. He can teach them that they can live without things they thought they needed. How might God teach a missionary these things?**

2. UGALI, CHAI, AND GROUND NUTS

MATERIALS

ugali, a pitcher of tea (hot or room temperature), hot milk in a thermos, ground ginger, shelled unsalted peanuts, paper plates, styrofoam cups, plastic spoons, paper towels, hand cleansing gel or wipes

Ugali Recipe—serves 8

1 1/2 cups water
1 cup white cornmeal
Bring water to a boil. Add cornmeal and stir constantly until thick as mashed potatoes.

DO: Ask students to clean their hands with gel or wipes. Give each student a paper plate and styrofoam cup. Fill one-fourth of each cup with tea. Then pour hot milk into the tea to fill the cups about halfway. Sprinkle a bit of ground ginger on top. Ask the students to gently stir this drink. Tell them this is Kenyan *chai* (pronounced "ch + eye"). Give each of them a small serving of *ugali* (oo-gah'-lee) and a handful of peanuts, called "ground nuts" in Kenya. To be truly Kenyan, eat with your fingers. Kenyans take a little of the ugali, roll it in their hands to form a small ball, then dip it into their other food.

DISCUSS: While students eat, ask if they've ever had any of these foods before. Ask: **Which of these foods do you like best? Which do you like least?** Tell the students that many people in Kenya eat only one meal a day, because they don't have enough food. The women often cook outdoors over a charcoal stove called a "jeé-ko." Ask: **What could God teach a missionary to Kenya?** (He can teach them to trust in him and depend on him. He can teach them that people who are poor can be rich in faith. He can teach them that life's importance is in people, not things. He can teach them that they can live without things they thought they needed.) **Why would God want to teach missionaries as well as the people he has sent them to?**

3. DANCING THE MASAI AND THE LUHYA

MATERIALS

a copy of the Dances of the Masai and Luhya (page 83)

NOTE: The following dances are like what we would call kinesthetics or exercises. These dances are celebratory in nature and are as basic to tribal identity as language or dress. It's not uncommon for Kenyan Christians to include these dances in church worship and other gatherings.

DO: Practice these two dances before class so that you can help your students learn them. Then practice the dances with your students. As you get comfortable with the movements, you can call out the names of the dances at random and let the students do the dance. Stop in time to have a discussion.

DISCUSS: Tell the students that the names of the dances are actually the names of the tribes that do those dances. The Masai are one tribe; the Luhya are another tribe. Each tribe has its own language, dress, dance, and religion. Ask: **Why do people in Africa need to know Jesus? What would you tell them about Jesus? What can we do to help if we can't go there?** (We can give and pray.) **What can God teach missionaries while they are in other countries?** (He can teach them to depend on him. He can teach them that people who are poor can be rich in faith. He can teach them that life's importance is in people, not things. He can teach them that they can live without things they thought they needed.) **Why might a missionary want to study his Bible and get to know God even better while he's on a mission?**

DISCOVERERS' DEBRIEFING

If you have time to review, gather as a large group and discuss your young discoverers' findings. Ask the following questions:

- **What is the most interesting thing you discovered today?**
- **What did you learn today that you did not know before?**
- **How does missions work bless the people of other nations?**
- **How can missions work bless the missionaries?**
- **What could God teach a missionary?**
- **What would you tell people in Africa about Jesus?**
- **What can we do to help if we can't go there?**

Review the Scripture for today. Pray, asking God to draw the nations of Africa to Jesus. Ask God to bless the missionaries who are in Africa and teach them more about him.

Dear friends,

My family and I moved to Kenya, Africa several years ago to be missionaries there. The thing I enjoy most about Kenya is that the people here are so friendly. I have friends my age. We like to play soccer and freeze tag.

My favorite food from Kenya is green grams with chapatis. Green grams are mung beans. Chapatis are like pancakes, but bigger and not sweet. They are like big tortillas, but thicker and a little oily.

My house is like a house in America, except that it has a wall around the yard and a gate that is guarded at night. We have a garden in the back yard. Out in the country, called the "bush," many people build houses of mud, cow dung, and straw.

We have matatus for public transportation. That is a pickup truck with a topper that takes about 25 people all crowded in together. Not very comfortable! Lots of people just walk.

My daddy works to build and remodel buildings at a Christian school that helps pastors and leaders learn the truth about God.

Kenya feels like home to me. I hope you enjoy learning about this country.

Your friend,

Shaun
Kitale, Kenya, Africa

Dances of the Masai and Luya

The Masai (mah-si')

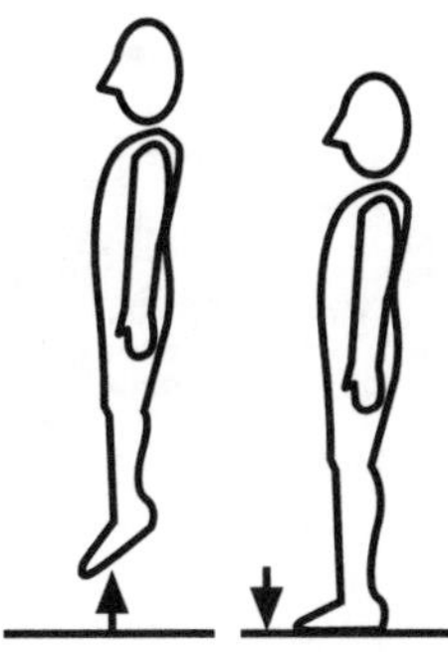

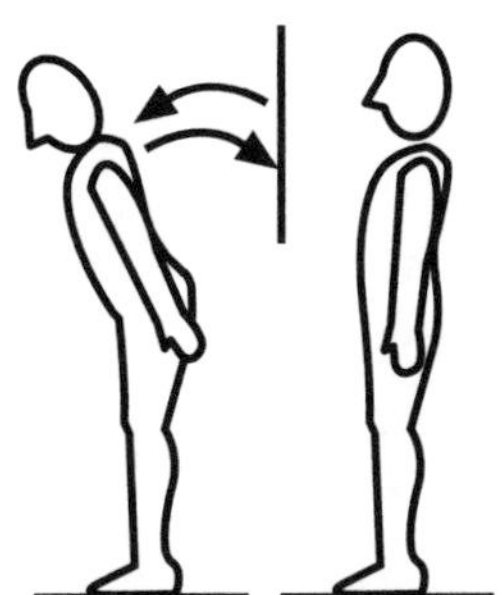

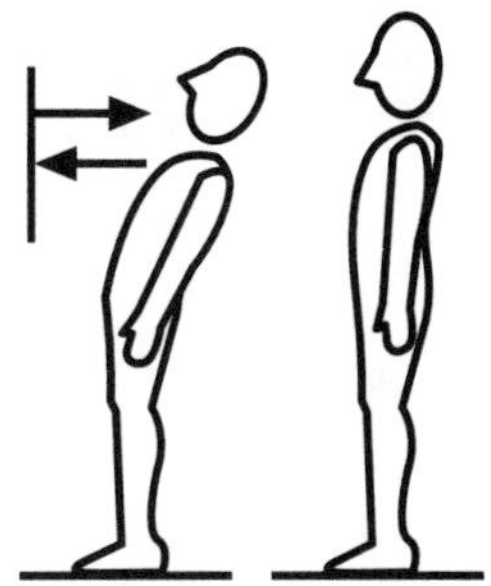

The rhythm is 1-2-3-4 1-2-3-4:
1—Jump Up 2—Land

Hands at your side, legs straight, jump as high as you can. Land back on both feet.

3—Lean forward

With legs and back straight, arms to your side, lean forward, then straighten up.

4—Lean back

Same posture: lean back, then straighten up.

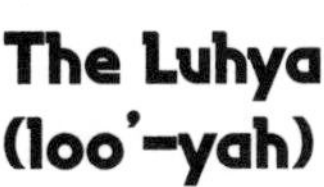

The Luhya (loo'-yah)

Foot pattern:
Stand straight. Keeping knees stiff, slide first the right foot back and return it to beginning position. Then slide the left foot back and return it to beginning position. This will be the foot movement for the dance, repeating over and over: right, left, right, left.

Hand pattern:
While feet go right, left once, bring the right arm around from side to front in a circular motion as if stirring a big pot. When the feet go right, left a second time, the left arm circles around in the same way. Continue right, left. For each two feet moves, one arm stirs.
Arms: stir right; stir left.
Feet: right, left; right, left.

Missions in Oceania

Scripture

"Exalt the name of the Lord, the God of Israel, in the islands of the sea." *Isaiah 24:15b, NIV*

Goal

Gain a vision of giving, praying, and going to Australia and the Pacific islands.

Learn that some missionaries write the Bible in tribal languages which have never been written down before.

INTRODUCTION

Make two copies and cut out the stamps from Stamps of the Nations (page 90). Mix the stamps up. As students arrive, give each one a stamp. They must find the person who has the matching stamp. Then together they go to the world map and locate the country that their stamp comes from and name the continent that the country is in. Then together, they try to remember as much as they can of what they have learned about that country or continent.

DISCOVERY RALLY

Gather the students together in a large group in front of the world map.

WHAT'S THE GOOD WORD?

Choose a student to read the Scripture for the day.

THE CHALLENGE

If you've received any new e-mails or letters from missionaries the class has written to, read them at this time.

Before class, copy the letter from New Zealand (page 91) and put it in an envelope. Write on a chalkboard, dry erase board, or poster board the word: Taumata-whaka-tangi-hanga-koa-uauo-tamatea-turipu-kakapiki-maunga-horo-nuku-pokai-whenua-kita-natahu, New Zealand. Show this place name to the students and tell them that today they will be discovering an area of the world in which there is a place that has this name. It is the longest place name in the world. It means: "The place where Tamatea, the man with the big knees, who slid, climbed, and swallowed mountains, known as land eater, played his flute to his loved one." Ask everyone to try to say this place name together.

Point out New Zealand and other island nations on the world map. Tell students that this is a part of the world that some people call "Oceania." Tell the students that you have a letter to them from New Zealand. Give the envelope to a student and ask him or her to open the letter and read it to the class.

Ask: **What did you hear in the letter that sounded like our country? What did you hear that sounded different? What else might be different for a missionary from our country living in Oceania?** Now ask students what the Scripture for today was. If they can't remember it, ask someone to read it again. Tell the students that in their Discovery Centers today they will look at Oceania as a place where they can give, pray, and go.

PRAYER

DISCOVERY CENTERS

NOTE: If your church supports missionaries in Oceania, you may want to change Center #2 or Center #3, and let the students write letters to your missionaries. Gather the letters and send them this week. Or copy them and send them by e-mail. Perhaps your class will get a letter in reply!

1. PEACE BOOKMARK

MATERIALS

bookmarks from last week, markers, a piece of paper and marker for yourself

DO: Give the students their bookmarks. Write on your piece of paper the word "maluhia." Tell the students that this is the Hawaiian word for "peace." It is pronounced "mah-loo-hee'-ah." Ask them to say the word with you. Then ask them to write it on their bookmarks. Gather the bookmarks and keep them for next week.

Then help students learn how to say some words in Rapanui (rah-pah-noo'-ee), the language spoken on Easter Island. "How are you?" is "Pehe koe," pronounced "Pay-hay kaw'-ay." "Fine" is "Rivariva," pronounced "Ree-vah-ree'-vah." Practice saying these together. Then choose one student to go first. This student turns to the person on his left and says, "Pehe koe?" The student who received this greeting says, "Rivariva." Then that student turns to the person on her left and says, "Pehe koe?" Continue this way around the group.

DISCUSS: If your church supports missionaries in Oceania, this is a good time to talk about who they are. Show pictures of them if possible. Find their location on the map. Give a report about what God is doing in their area.

Tell the students that even though Hawaii is part of the United States, the native people group there are people from the Pacific Islands. This is why they still have a Hawaiian language. Also tell the students that over 300 million people in our world still don't have a way to write their own language. Ask: **How can these people learn about God? What would make it difficult for these people to grow in their knowledge about Jesus?** Tell them that some missionaries spend many years living with these people groups, figuring out what a tribe's language would look like in writing. Then these missionaries write the Bible in that language. Ask: **How do you think a missionary could figure out how to write a language that has never been written before?**

2. POSTCARDS

MATERIALS
6" x 4" unlined index cards, markers, crayons, or colored pencils

DO: Give each student an index card. Tell the students that these will be postcards representing the islands of Oceania. Ask them what comes into their minds when they think of these islands. You may suggest beaches, starfish, surfing, palm trees, colorful birds and flowers, rainbows, sunsets over the ocean, seashells, boats, fishing. Then ask them to design a picture about the islands on one side of the card. On the other side of the card, they write the Scripture for today, "Exalt the name of the Lord . . . in the islands of the sea" (Isaiah 24:15). Next, they choose the name of an island nation from the world map and write the verse again, inserting that name. For example, "Exalt the name of the Lord in Fiji."

DISCUSS: As the students design their cards, tell them about the Binumarion tribe from Papua New Guinea. Their tribe was growing smaller and smaller until there were only 112 of them left. They believed that God had made only men in the beginning. They believed that God had turned a man into a woman for punishment. So they decided that women were bad, and men should stay away from them. But then missionaries came. The missionaries listened carefully as the Binumarion people talked, and they figured out how to write down the Binumarion language. Then they wrote the Bible in this language and taught the people to read. The people were amazed. They read, "God created man in his own image—male and female he created them" Genesis 1:27. All the villages became excited. They now knew the truth. They started having families, and their tribe began growing again. Ask: **Why was life not working for this tribe before the missionaries came? What changed? Why? How can we help these islands if we can't go there? We can give and pray.**

3. TROPICAL FRUIT AND COCONUT PUDDING

MATERIALS

coconut pudding made from a mix, bananas, sliced kiwi fruit, pineapple chunks, mandarin oranges, cantaloupe chunks, disposable picnic bowls, plastic spoons, paper plates, a marker, knife for teacher's use, paper towels, hand cleansing gel or wipes

DO: Before class, mix the coconut pudding. Slice the fruit except the bananas. Write the following food names on the paper plates you'll be using to serve each kind of fruit: *maika* is a banana in Rapanui (Easter Island); *'anani* is an orange in Rapanui; *anana* is a pineapple in Rapanui; "rock melon" is a cantaloupe in Australia; and kiwi fruit is from New Zealand

As the students come to your group, ask them to wash their hands with the gel or wipes. Place some of each fruit on its plate, slicing at least one fresh banana for each group. Tell the students the names of the fruits and which countries use that name. Tell them that the islands grow many kinds of fruit. Coconut cream pudding or sauce is also a common food. Give each student some coconut pudding in a bowl. They can use the toothpicks to get chunks of fruits to put on top of their pudding before they eat.

DISCUSS: As the students eat, say: **We use the words "people groups" to mean groups of people who have the same native language and customs. There are many people groups who live in our nation.** Ask the students to name some of the people groups who live in our nation. Say: **Just as there are many people groups here, there are also different people groups living in other nations of the world. For example, in the island of Fiji, one people group is Hindi. They are people that came to the islands from India. There are many people groups that don't yet know about Jesus. They don't have Bibles. Some don't even have a written language.** Ask: **Does God care? Why or why not? What can we do about it? Give, pray, and go.**

DISCOVERERS' DEBRIEFING

If you have time to review, gather as a large group and discuss your young discoverers' findings. Ask the following questions:

- **What is the most interesting thing you discovered today?**
- **What did you learn today that you did not know before?**
- **How can people who don't even have a written language learn about God?**
- **How would a missionary figure out how to write a language that has never been written before?**
- **Why does life not work for people before they learn about God?**
- **How can we help the islands if we can't go there?**

Review the Scripture for today.

Pray, asking God to draw the people of Oceania to Jesus. Ask God to send missionaries to the people groups who have never heard of Jesus. Ask God to help us give, pray, and go.

Stamps of the Nations

Netherlands

Vietnam

Canada

Russia

Thailand

Germany

Sudan

Botswana

Uruguay

Mexico

Kenya

Denmark

South Africa

Greece

Egypt

Dear friends,

Our family went on a short-term mission trip to New Zealand. That means we didn't move to New Zealand. We were missionaries for just five weeks there. We taught children about Jesus, and we taught adults how to teach their children about Jesus. We didn't stay in one city. We traveled all over the country to different places.

One of the things we enjoyed most about New Zealand was the beautiful countryside. There were lots of green grassy hills with sheep all over them. Because New Zealand is in the southern half of the world, the farther you go north, the warmer it gets. The farther you go south, the colder it gets. And the seasons are the opposite of ours. We went to New Zealand when it was spring in the U.S. But in New Zealand, it was autumn. When we went to the south island, it got quite cold. But up on the north island, we went to the beach, and there were tropical plants like there are in Hawaii.

One of our favorite foods was hamburgers made the New Zealand way: with slices of beets on them! They also had lots of kiwi fruit (which they cut in half and scoop out with a spoon), and sweet potatoes, called *kumara*. They have different kinds of drinks there, too. We liked a lemon-lime drink the best. They have lots of different kinds of candy, too. Crunchie bars were our favorite!

We were invited to visit some boys who were our age. They taught us to play rugby, which is a little like our football, but a lot rougher. We got very muddy! They also play a lot of soccer.

Some people can't leave their jobs or families to go and live for a long time in other countries as missionaries. So going on a short-term mission trip can be just the right way for them to be a missionary! Maybe you can be a short-term missionary someday.

Your friends,

Raygan and Heath
New Zealand

Session 13

Start Where You Are

Scripture

"May your ways be known throughout the earth, your saving power among people everywhere."
Psalm 67:2, NLT

Goal

Learn that our mission can start today where we are with the people we know and meet.
Learn that we can give, pray, and go.

INTRODUCTION

As students arrive, give each one a piece of paper. Ask them to draw maps of their own neighborhoods.

DISCOVERY RALLY

Gather the students together in a large group in front of the world map.

WHAT'S THE GOOD WORD?

Choose a student to read the Scripture for the day.

THE CHALLENGE

If you've received any new e-mails or letters from missionaries the class has written to, read them at this time.

Ask: **If you were going to be a missionary and could choose right now where in the world you wanted to go, which nation would you choose? Why?** Say: **We've been talking about sending missionaries from our country into the world. Could other nations send missionaries to the United States? Why or why not?** Tell students that a man and his wife came from the island of New Zealand to the United States to preach in a church here. A couple from South Africa came to teach and preach in the United States. A South African singing group came to spread God's word through the United States. Ask why.

Tell the students that in their Discovery Centers today they will find out about how their mission can start now with the people they meet each day.

PRAYER

DISCOVERY CENTERS

1. PEACE BOOKMARK

MATERIALS

the students' bookmarks, markers or pens, transparent adhesive shelf paper, scissors

DO: Give the students their bookmarks. If they have space left on the back of the bookmark, ask them to write "Give—Pray—Go" in that space. Then stretch some transparent adhesive shelf paper on a table, sticky side up. Carefully peel off the backing. Students lay their bookmarks face down on the adhesive. Cut the adhesive paper to separate the bookmarks. Let the students trim the excess adhesive paper off of their bookmarks. Then do the same with the backs of their bookmarks so that both sides are laminated. Let the students take these home today.

DISCUSS: Ask: **What do we mean when we say "Give-Pray-Go"? How can you give? How can you pray? How can you go? Do you have to go to a different nation? How can you be a missionary here in your own country? What is a mission? Can a writer have a mission? Can a computer programmer have a mission? How? What is the mission of every follower of Jesus?**

2. SWITCHING ON THE LIGHT

MATERIALS

a switchplate for each student, Sculpey brand modeling clay in a variety of colors, paper plates, wax paper, a rolling pin, plastic knives, round toothpicks, markers, hand cleaning gel or wipes, optional: an oven and baking sheet, pot holder, a Bible

DO: Give each student a piece of wax paper. Let each student take a bit of the colors he wants for his switchplate cover. Students knead their chosen colors together to get a marbled ball of clay. Then they flatten the clay on the wax paper and roll it thin with a rolling pin. Now give each student a switchplate. Students write their name on the back of the switchplate with a marker. Then they press the front of the switchplate onto the clay and cut the excess clay from around the edges of the switchplate and from the hole in the center. Now they gently remove the switch plate from the wax paper. They clear the clay from the holes in the switch plate using the toothpicks. Give each student a paper plate. Ask them to write on the plate, "Bake for 15 minutes at 250 degrees." They may take these home and bake them. Students clean their hands with the gel or wipes.

OPTION: If you have access to an oven, set it to 250 degrees before you start the activity. When the switchplates are covered with clay, ask students to place the switchplates on a baking sheet. Bake them for 15 minutes at 250 degrees. They can bake while the students go to their next center.

DISCUSS: Ask someone to read Matthew 5:14-16. Say: **This verse tells us one way to communicate the good news about Jesus to others. What is it?** Remind the students that our actions often speak louder than our words. Ask: **What are some things you can do, without even speaking, that will tell others about Jesus? What are some places you go each week? How can you shine Jesus' light in those places?** Say: **Put the switchplate on the light switch in your room if you can. Then every time you turn your light on, remember that you are the light of the world. It is your good deeds that show people what Jesus is like.**

3. POPCORN FEST

MATERIALS

plain popcorn (you can pop it in class if you want), a microwave oven or toaster oven or hot plate and pan for melting butter, pot holder, grated parmesan cheese, butter, peanut butter, orange juice, chili powder, microwavable bowls, plastic spoons, paper bowls, paper towels, hand cleaning gel or wipes

DO: Bring the popcorn or pop it in class. Students can help you put the parmesan cheese in a bowl. In one bowl, mix equal amounts of peanut butter and butter, melt it, and stir it together. In another, mix orange juice with butter. In another, mix a bit of chili powder with butter. And provide a bowl of plain butter. Place a spoon in each bowl. After each student gets a paper bowl with popcorn in it, they drizzle the topping of their choice on the popcorn. They may try several different toppings.

DISCUSS: Tell the students that popcorn is an American food. The native Americans were popping popcorn long before other settlers arrived in the Americas. Ask: **What was the mission of some of the first settlers in America? Their mission was to bring God's good news to America.** Ask: **Do you think that there may still be people in America who haven't heard about Jesus? Explain.** Remind students that they can start their mission now with the people they see each day. Ask: **What is the message about Jesus?** As the students eat, teach them the following way to tell about salvation with hand motions. (If your students have already gone through the Salvation quarter of the Foundations curriculum, this will be review for them.)

God is perfect. *(point up to God)*

I am not. *(point to self)*

But Jesus came to take the blame. *(form a J)*

He died on the cross, punished for my sins. *(form a cross)*

Now I can be perfect, forgiven and blameless. *(put hands out, palms up)*

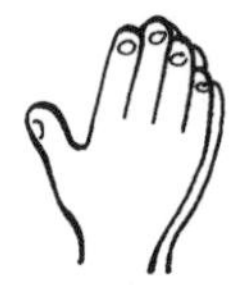

All I have to do is ask. *(form praying hands)*

DISCOVERERS' DEBRIEFING

If you have time to review, gather as a large group and discuss your young discoverers' findings. Ask the following questions:

- **What is the most interesting thing you discovered today?**
- **What did you learn today that you did not know before?**
- **What do we mean when we say "Give-Pray-Go"? How can you give? How can you pray? How can you go?**
- **How can you be a missionary in your own country?**
- **What did Jesus mean when he said, "You are the light of the world?"**
- **What are some things you can do, without even speaking, that will tell others about Jesus?**
- **What is the message about Jesus?**

Review the Scripture for today.

Pray, thanking God for loving us so that we can love others. Ask God to draw the people around us to Jesus. Ask him to help us give, pray, and go.